DESIGNING YOUR LIFE WITH DESIGNER FOODS: THE FACTS ABOUT PHYTOCHEMICALS

Dr. Neecie Moore

Charis Publishing Co.

Published by Charis Publishing Co.
P. O. Box 740607
Dallas, TX 75374

All rights reserved. No part of this book may be reproduced in any form without written permission from Charis Publishing Co. This book is intended to be a reference only. It is not to be used for diagnosis or treatment of disease. Before making changes in your diet, your medication or your exercise program, consult with your physician.

Copyright © 1996 by Charis Publishing Co.
Cover by Mickey Torres
Hair by Sandi Narramore of Hair Flaire, Richardson, TX

Printed in the United States of America
ISBN: 0-9647546-2-2
Dr. Neecie Moore
Designing Your Life with Designer Foods:
The Facts about Phtyochemicals
First Edition
$12.95 Softcover

DEDICATION

Growing up for me was special in many ways.
Special because my best friend lived just
down the hall from me.

She let me sleep with her when I was afraid;
she took up for me when I was in trouble;
she befriended and awed every teacher in our schools two
years ahead of me to blaze a path of respect for me;
she taught me all the tricks of success in the band
and in clubs; she got me dates;
she taught me to sneak ice cream cones
from the Dairy Queen
when we were supposed to be on diets.

One of the saddest days of my life was when
she left for college.
Yet she never left my heart.

From the time we were toddlers
until the last few years, people
thought we were twins. Our dad called
us both "sister" so he didn't have to
figure out which one was which.

She has produced the four greatest joys of my life:
KIMBERLY, JASON, PAUL AND REBEKAH.
She has let her children be like my very own.

I dedicate this book to my
very best friend, my precious sister
RUANA GENEAN GRACE.

I LOVE YOU!

ACKNOWLEDGEMENTS

I have so many wonderful friends, family members, and colleagues to thank for support and assistance throughout his project:

RED AND SISSIE MOORE, my wonderful parents, for giving me life and love;

DR. ROBERT R. SCHEINBERG for single-handedly putting me back together after I was hit by a moving vehicle (even though we thought all the king's horses and all the king's men couldn't put me together again);

DENICE FARRAR for being my own special angel and taking such great care of me;

DALE SMITH, SARA WEEKS-SMITH, "THE CARRIE, KARI, AND JERRY SHOW," SCOTT, STEVE, RACHEL, CHRISTINE, ELLEN, CHANDLER, SUSIE ISHIBASHI, RANDALL SIMPSON, AMBER WIRTZ, RENEE ALSCHBACH, VICKI KOCH, SANDRA DeVAULT, LINDA BERSON and all the great folks at the Cooper Aerobic Center Southwest Physical Therapy for providing "torture with a smile" and never giving up on me;

And to my recovering partners in therapy at Southwest Physical Therapy who became like family: GREG DULCIE, KARLA MUSSETTER, CARL BAILEY, KIM HARVEL, VALERIE SHEFFIELD, LINDA TAYLOR, BROOKE BURNS, SHIRLEY, ERIC, PAUL, NANCY and many others;

The great folks at the SPA AT THE DORAL in Miami for being such an integral part of my recovery; special thanks to MONICA; also to HELEN, TAMMY, ANA, PRECIOUS SANDRA (for the great hair and make up), REBECCA, ROBERTA, NORELLA, PEDRO, HUMBERTO, CHARLOTTE, KYLE; and to my Doral buddies, LINDA RAE SWANSON and JERI TOMPKINS;

RICHARDSON PUBLIC LIBRARY for helping me obtain some of my research material;

BRENT BOULDIN, my delightful cousin, for encouragement, advice, laughs, and understanding;

Sam and Linda Caster and Don and Lydia Herndon for their friendship and prayers;

C.C. Brown for her hard work on reading, editing and re-reading this book;

CHUCK GRACE, my brother-in-law, for being more helpful and loving to my sister so I'd mention him in my book;

HAROLD WILLIS for the excellent assistance with editing;

Drs. Reg and Candi McDaniel, Bill and Donna Fioretti, Skip Fioretti, Pat Cobb, Missy and the other fine folks in Grand Prairie;

REVA AND BOB; NEVA; CHERYL AND DICK; LOWELL AND MARY ANN; ANNE AND DALE; WILL AND WILMA for welcoming me, for all the great stories, and for the walks on the "farm;"

ANNE AND DALE; DAVID; MARGUERITE; LAURA, GEORGE AND RACHEL for the hikes in the mountains, for the search for dinosuar bones, and for all the laughs;

DR. SAM HARVEY AND DR. NADINE PALAU for support, direction and guidance;

ANTHONY ROBBINS who taught me to change my fear into power in the fire-walk experience;

CAROL AND ANDY HOLT; PAT AND GLEN HOLT; JANIS AND SKIP GREEN; AND MOMSY for being so good to me and loving me through thick and thin;

PAUL AND VICKY BISCHOFF for sharing the greatest girls in the world with me and doing such a wonderful job with them;

SIDNEY AND LINDA BRANDON for believing me and believing in me;

MY FIRSTERS: MARY ELLEN, GINNY, SUSAN, SHARI and ANITA for teaching the meaning of real friendship;

THE JOY LUCK INVESTMENT CLUB for all the great lunches, laughs and learnin';

ELLEN MORGAN, DR. STERLING SIGHTLER, CARLENE NORWOOD, CAROLYN HANCOCK, JUDY, DONNA BRUCE AND PATTI for being such good freinds to my mother and our family;

KAY JACKSON for being the best friend I could ever have;

JILL AND SARAH HOLT for loving me as their aunt, no matter what; and

ANDREA, KELLI, AND COLLEEN HOLT for being my precious girls.

IN SPECIAL RECOGNITION:

Of my wonderful family for coming from all over the country for a "Sherron Family Reunion." John and Jamille Maher (my ancient cousin and her husband) from Virginia; Tina, Wes and Shelby Frasard from North Carolina; Cindi, Eddie and Shane Morris from Arkansas; Brent Bouldin from Seattle, Washington; Melissa Evans, Linda Lovelady, Jim and Jennifer Russell from East Texas; Kimberly and Rodney Parker from Texas; my bushka, Rebekah Grace from Louisiana who was already here to spend the summer with me; and my dad, "Red," my mom, "Sissie," and my sister, Ruana Grace from Louisiana.

SPECIAL THANKS TO:

GARY L. WATSON

For believing in my projects
and for all the love and support in the process.
And thanks to Ben and Jack
for being a part of one
of the most important moments
of my life!

IN LOVING MEMORY OF

Aunt Lou Bledsoe

and

Bruce Davis;

Fric and Frac
(who brought us much joy)

and Cracker Jack
(who truly was my best friend for the last nine years)

TABLE OF CONTENTS

1. Prevention & Natural Medicine 1
   Our Population & a Need for Pharmaceuticals Increases. . . 3
   Pharmaceutical Companies and Their Ad Campaigns 4
   Taking Responsibility for Health and Prevention 6
   Wholistic Health 7
   Alternative Medicine 9
2. Phytochemicals: What They Are & What They Do 10
   The Study of Plants 11
   Growth in the Field of Phytochemistry 12
   The Importance of Phytochemicals 13
   A Five Year Study of Phytochemicals 14
   The Biotechnological Industry Designs Foods 15
   Designer Foods 16
3. Fruits & Vegetables. 19
   Do We Eat as We Should for the Sake of Our Health? . . . 21
   Eating Sensibly for the Sake of Our Health 22
   The 5-a-Day Program 23
   Diets of American Kids and Teens 23
   Educating Kids, Teens and Their Parents. 25
4. Phytochemicals in Fruits & Vegetables 27
   Tomatoes. 28
   Hot Peppers 29
   Carrots 30

Cruciferous Vegetables: Broccoli, Brussels Sprouts,
Cabbage, Kale, Turnips, Cauliflower and Turnip Greens ... 31
Citris Fruits: Oranges, Lemons and Grapefruits 34
Papayas 35
Raspberries, Grapes, Strawberries and Blueberries 36
Apples 37
Artichokes 38
Onions 39

5. Garlic: The Miracle Plant 43
Historical Uses of Garlic 44
Phytochemicals in Garlic 45
Garlic and Arthritis 45
Garlic and Blood Pressure 46
Garlic and The Nursing Mother 46
Garlic and Cancer 47
Garlic's Effect on Stomach and Colon Cancer 48
Garlic as an Antibacterial 48
Garlic and Parasites 49
Garlic and Cholesterol Levels 49
Garlic as an Antiflatulent 50
Garlic and Heart Disease 50
Garlic and The Immune System 51
Garlic and AIDS 51
Garlic as an Antibiotic 52
Using Garlic With Colds and Flu 52
Garlic and Yeast Infections 52
Garlic's Antimicrobial Properties 53

    Garlic as an Antidepressant 53
    Garlic and Ulcers 54
    The List of Benefits Goes On 54
6. Cancer Prevention 56
    Cancer Reduction Through Dietary Changes 57
    The Diet and Cancer Project 57
    Diet and Tumor Prevention 58
    Are We Responsible With Our Diet and Health Care? . . . 59
    Breast Cancer Prevention 60
    Phytochemicals Block Carcinogens 61
    Sulphoraphane as a Cancer Preventative 61
    Cartenoids as a Cancer Preventative 62
    Folic Acid as a Cancer Preventative 62
    Allixin as a Cancer Preventative 63
    Calcium as a Cancer Preventative 63
    Flavonoids as a Cancer Preventative 64
    Other Cancer-Preventing Phytochemicals 64
7. Lung Cancer: The Preventative Effect
    of Fruits & Vegetables 66
    Smokers Eat Less Fruits and Vegetables 68
    Vitamin C Protects the Lungs 68
    Stop Smoking! 69
    Fruit and Vegetable Consumption
    Lowers Risk of Lung Cancer 70
    Beta Carotene and Lung Cancer 70
    Fruits And Vegetables in the Treatment of Lung Cancer . . . 72
    It Doesn't Take Much 73

8. Colon Cancer: The Effects of Fruits & Vegetables. 74
   A Hopeful Note About Colon Cancer Preventation 75
   Fruits and Vegetables Protect Against Colon Cancer 76
   Beta Carotene and Colon Cancer. 76
   Dietary Predictors of Colon Cancer. 77
   Cabbage and Other Cruciferous Vegetables
   As Colon Cancer Preventatives. 78
   Garlic and Colon Cancer 78
   Pectin as a Preventative Of Colon Cancer. 78
9. Breast Cancer: Diet-Related Prevention And Treatment . . 80
   Defending Yourself Against Breast Cancer 81
   Lowering the intake of Fat to Reduce
   the Risk of Breast Cancer 81
   Fruits and Vegetables as a Line of Defense
   Against Breast Cancer. 82
   Cruciferous Vegetables and Breast Cancer. 83
   Beans and Breast Cancer. 84
   Green Vegetables and Breast Cancer. 84
   Garlic and Breast Cancer 84
   Selenium and Breast Cancer 85
   Fruits & Vegetables Prevent Spreading of Breast Cancer . . 86
10. Prostate, Stomach, Pancreatic & Skin Cancers:
    Can Fruits & Vegetables Help?. 87
    Prostate Cancer 87
    Stomach Cancer 89
    Pancreatic Cancer 91
    Skin Cancer. 92

11. Heart Problems: Cardiovascular Disease,
    Blood Pressure & Cholesterol.................. 95
    Vegetarians and Heart Disease 96
    High Blood Pressure and Cholesterol Problems 97
    Angina.. 97
    Garlic and Heart Disease 98
    Hypertension: High Blood Pressure................ 99
    Controlling Blood Pressure with Fruits and Vegetables ... 99
    Vitamin C and High Blood Pressure 100
    Calcium and High Sodium Levels: No More Salt?....... 100
    Potassium and High Blood Pressure................. 101
    Celery and High Blood Pressure 102
    Garlic and High Blood Pressure.................... 102
    Cayenne Pepper and High Blood Pressure............ 103
    A Macrobiotic Diet and High Blood Pressure 103
    Cholesterol Levels.............................. 104
    The Impact of Fruits and Vegetables on
    Cholesterol Levels.............................. 105
    Garlic and Cholesterol Levels 106
    Onions and Cholesterol Levels 106
    Avacados and Cholesterol Levels................... 107
    Apples and Cholesterol Levels..................... 107
12. Depression and Seasonal Affective Disorder (SAD)..... 109
    How Food and Diet Affects Your Mood.............. 110
    Fruits And Vegetables Affect Levels of Depression 112
    Depression: An Imbalance of Neurotransmitters
    in the Brain 112

Folic Acid and its Effect on Depression 113
Endorphin Levels and Depression 114
Chili Peppers as an Antidepressant 114
Vitamin C and Depression. 115
Garlic and Depression. 115
Onions as an Antianxiety Agent. 116
Amino Acids as Antidepressants 116
Avoid Tap Water to Avoid Depression. 117
Exercise, Seratonin and Depression. 117
Seasonal Affective Disorder. 118
Preventing Depression, Anxiety and Stress. 120

13. Antioxidants vs. Free Radicals:
   The Battle Fruits & Vegetables Can Win 121
   What Are Free Radicals? 122
   Free Radicals as "Good Guys". 122
   Where Do Free Radicals Come From? 123
   What Are Antioxidants? 124
   Atherosclerosis 125
   Heart Disease 126
   Cancer 126
   AIDS 128
   Cataracts. 128
   Arthritis 129
   Parkinson's Disease 129
   Why Should We Take Antioxidants? 130
   What Foods Contain Antioxidants? 131

14. A Prescription for a Healthy, Happy Life 134

Rx #1 — Choose Wellness as a Way of Life 135
Rx #2 — Have Fun! And Laugh!. 136
Rx #3 — Exercise Moderately and Regularly. 136
Rx #4 — Get Adequate Rest 137
Rx #5 — Get Your Spiritual Life in Order. 138
Rx #6 — Go an Extra Mile 138
Rx #7: — Increase Your Intake of Fruits and
   Vegetables (Improve Your Diet and Intake Of
   Supplements) 139
Bibilography. 141
Index. 153

INTRODUCTION

> "A sensible life-style, with good healthy food, regular moderate exercise and restful sleep is still the best medicine for many problems."
> —Linda Rector-Page, 1992

More than 2000 years ago, Hippocrates (the Father of Medicine) proclaimed: "Let food be your medicine and medicine be your food." Hmmm. What an interesting thought. I can imagine that he never envisioned that we would be driving through McDonald's, Wendy's, Burger King, Taco Bell and Arby's to get our "medicine." I can also imagine that he never thought we would spend so much time at Eckerd's, Wal-Mart, Tom Thumb-Page and other pharmacies awaiting prescriptions for our "food."

Our bodies are amazing creations. However, after years of misuse and abuse, they may not function as amazingly as they were created to function. In the Himalayan mountains, there is a group of people who are a great testimony of the fullness and longevity of life when bodies are not misused and abused. Among the Hunzans, there are no doctors, and there are no childhood diseases. There is very little infant mortality, and people live to ripe old ages. Their ninety-year-old men are still fathering children and rearing families. There are no crime rates, making jails and policemen needless. There are virtually no divorces. "The people live long, happy, satisfying, productive lives in harmony with themselves, each other, and their environment. They enjoy life and health" (Morter, 1990). This is a wonderful illustration of how our bodies could live and function much longer than we now seem to believe they can, if we "provide it the proper exercise, serenity, diet, and environment" (Morter, 1990).

This definitely concurs with what our Father of Medicine was writing about over 2000 years ago. In speaking about the writings of Hippocrates, Airola stated: "Diseases are of man's own making and are the end result of a long-time abuse in the form of poor living habits, faulty nutrition and other health-destroying environmental problems" (Airola, 1971, p. 176).

JUST ANOTHER ORDINARY DAY

Take a moment to consider a day of your life. Up when the alarm goes off . . . get yourself (and your children, if you have them) ready for school, work, or whatever is on your schedule for the day . . . jump in the car, or on the bus, or on the subway, to reach your destination . . . fight traffic, hustle to get there on time . . . deal with a stressful day at work . . . cope by consuming massive amounts of caffeine to stay awake or by consuming cookies or chips to comfort yourself through the stress . . . rush to fight traffic again . . . stop by the cleaners, the grocery store, and whatever other errands might be on the list for the day . . . arrive home to check the mail and find a pile of bills . . . listen to the messages on the answering machine and find out what else your church needs for you to do for the bazaar on Saturday, who needs you to volunteer for the local fund raiser, where you need to transport your children for the afternoon as their local taxi service . . . change clothes . . . prepare for an evening of activity, obligation, shuttle service, involvement in children's/other family members' activities . . . rush home . . . shower . . . EXHAUSTION! Yet there is still laundry to be done, lawns to be mowed, notes to be written, bills to be paid . . . and you hope to find time to pray and/or meditate?

Our lives have certainly become hectic and frantic. We no longer live life . . . life lives us. And we hang on for dear life.

A SPIRITUAL AWAKENING

I had an incredibly spiritual experience last year, which will be the springboard for my next book; a book about my personal journey . . . about determining what matters in life, and how to live life with passion and purpose. I had been to a doctor's appointment south of Dallas and was rushing back to my North Dallas office to have a session with a family that I had scheduled for an appointment and who I envisioned already in my waiting room waiting for me. I was running slightly behind my planned schedule, but knew if I hurried, I could make it on time. I was stressed with some information

I had received from my doctor, stressed that traffic was moving a bit slower than I had expected and was anxious to do the session with the family awaiting me in my office. Then the inevitable happened . . . traffic STOPPED! And it stopped in what, for me, was the most dreaded spot in all of Dallas. You see, down under those bridges in the downtown area of Dallas, I knew that there were myriads of "street people" living in cardboard houses. My heart breaks and aches to see their living circumstances, and I certainly didn't want to stop on top of a huge bridge to look down upon that scene in the midst of my stress. I was careful to look straight ahead. The traffic didn't budge. I sat . . . and sat. I phoned my office from my car to inform them I was delayed in traffic. My family had indeed arrived for their scheduled appointment, and there were several urgent messages to handle. My stress level mounted. I still refused to look down below the bridge. I sat . . . and sat. Finally, I accidentally allowed my eyes to wander to my left and down, almost as if they couldn't resist.

Much to my surprise, a miracle began in me at that very second. You see, when I glanced down, indeed there were cardboard houses, but there was something else that I never expected to see. It was a chilly, damp day . . . the kind I hate because I feel cold to the bone. My heater was on high, yet I couldn't seem to get warm. But below me, I saw a group of people, sitting around a fire in make-shift chairs made of crates, stumps and buckets. They were all laughing and talking and seemingly having a wonderful time of fellowship. I had to ask myself . . . who was "living life" in this situation? Was it me, sitting in halted traffic . . . stressed out? Or was it them sitting around their home fire enjoying the day despite the dampness? It certainly appeared to me that there was a warmth among them that the heater in my car couldn't provide.

Dr. Deepak Chopra had great insight by listing what is required to live a healthy life. The list certainly goes far beyond what we normally consider when we think of health. "Thus, a healthy life . . . demands the following: fresh food; pure water and air; sunlight; moderate exercise; balanced, refined breath; nonviolent behavior and a reverence for life; and loving, positive emotions" (Chopra, 1993, 264).

1 Prevention & Natural Medicine

> "Plants and people share
> the most essential element of all:
> the spark of life."
> — Linda Rector-Page, 1992

Health and health care are concerns that affect every one of us. Health care accounts for 12 percent of the gross national product (GNP). Yet there are approximately 37 million Americans who still have no health insurance (De Schepper, 1993). The Public Citizen's Health Research Group found that an average of 100,000 Americans monthly have lost their health insurance for each of the last five years. According to the same report, "if current trends continue, more than 43 million Americans will not have health insur-

The Facts About Phytochemicals

ance by the end of 1996" *(University of California at Berkeley Wellness Letter,* November, 1995). Some even say that this further indicates that health care in America is a "rich man's privilege." And health care costs continue to rise in an endless cycle. Health care costs rise because physicians must increase their charges for time spent with patients in order to account for the massive amounts of time spent on paperwork, reports and red tape required from insurance companies and to contend with managed care headaches. At the same time, malpractice insurance rates are skyrocketing. All of these costs figure into the rising costs of our health care.

Health care costs worldwide have passed $700 billion. And reportedly, the costs will exceed $1 trillion by the turn of the century (Chopra, 1993). One trillion is such an incredible number, it is hard to even imagine how many zeros make a trillion. (One trillion dollars is $1,000,000,000,000.— twelve zeros!)

One major part of health care costs is pharmaceuticals. Anytime most of us become ill or experience ailments, our first thoughts seem to automatically be directed to over-the-counter or prescription drugs. For most persons in our country, pharmaceuticals are easily obtained by a trip to the drug store (for over-the-counter drugs) or a trip to the doctor's office or health clinic (for prescription drugs). Currently, 80 percent of pharmaceuticals are consumed by 20 percent of the world's population, which some scientists call the 20/80 inverse ratio (Wijesekera, 1991).

OUR POPULATION AND NEED FOR PHARMACEUTICALS INCREASES

It is predicted that the world's population will surpass 7.5 billion by the year 2020. Currently, 75 percent of the world's population lives in the "developing world," or the part of the world often referred to as "third-world" countries. It is projected that an even larger percentage of the population will be in the "developing world" by the turn of the century. If these countries had the financial and logistical means to obtain the pharmaceuticals at the same per capita consumption rate as the rest of the world, their pharmaceutical costs alone would exceed $200 billion by the year 2020. That is more than the global consumption of pharmaceuticals at this time (Wijesekera, 1991).

In the early 1900s, developing pharmaceuticals and the medical profession worked hand in hand as an effective team. The doctor diagnosed and prescribed; and the "pills" provided the cure. Dr. Lendon H. Smith summarized the situation accurately: "The detective work was fun, the results were usually predictable and the patients were gratified because they got well so rapidly. But no one even considered those time-honored, natural, herbal, nutritional methods of getting well until people began to notice the nasty side effects and uncomfortable allergies from these 'miracle drugs'" (Heinerman, 1988).

Truly, for a time, it seemed that all considerations for natural healing vanished as the pharmaceutical industry flourished. But today, despite the growth in the pharmaceutical industry, "a substantial fraction of the world's population continues to use natural products, especially medicinal plant extracts, in helping control infectious diseases" (Hudson & Towers, 1991, p. 182).

PHARMACEUTICAL COMPANIES AND THEIR AD CAMPAIGNS

Have you ever considered how a physician keeps up with the countless numbers of new pharmaceutical drugs as they are approved by the FDA and brought to market? One of the ways is reading professional journals, the *Wall Street Journal* and other written material that provides updates. However, perhaps the most pervasive distribution of this information is done by the pharmaceutical companies, the companies that manufacture and sell the approved drugs.

Physicians are inundated by these companies with ads, visits from sales reps, and mailed incentives. For example, the next time you are in your doctor's office, note the Kleenex box and what drug it is advertising; note the candy dish and which company it is compliments of; note the pads of paper and whose name is on top of them; note the pens and which pharmaceutical companies they advertise. Pharmaceutical companies wage a marketing campaign to get physicians to prescribe their drug, just as soft drink companies, fast-food restaurants, and cologne manufacturers lull you into drinking their products, driving through their windows and spraying on their life-changing scents during commercial breaks, as you watch *PrimeTime Live*, the news, or your favorite sitcom on television.

Unfortunately, these companies do not always present their products accurately. The University of California at Los Angeles (UCLA) conducted a study regarding the advertising and marketing practices of pharmaceutical companies. The results were published in the *Annals of Internal Medicine* in June of 1992. The study found that more than 60 percent of the advertisements studied were either in direct violation of federal regulations and needed to be removed from the market, or that they were in need of major revision to meet federal regulations.

This is not to say that there is no value in pharmaceuticals. And there is certainly value in the continuing development of those drugs which can provide health benefits. Through the years, great hope has been placed in prolonging life and healing the sick as pharmaceutical development occurred.

However, as new pharmaceuticals were developed, the focus on natural healing and remedies seemed to diminish. We began giving doctors total control of our bodies and our health. It became obvious early in the twentieth century that we were rewarding doctors for treating illness rather than for promoting health. "Our society has allowed the entire health care industry to become so powerful and so disproportionately lucrative that it is now the business of illness rather than health" (Rector-Page, 1992, p. 8).

The Facts About Phytochemicals

TAKING RESPONSIBILITY FOR HEALTH AND PREVENTION

Many of us tend to blame health care costs on doctors; however, it is not the doctors alone who created this problem. We participate in and support the system that has led to this situation. How? . . . you might ask. I see the "why" demonstrated quite often in my practice as a marriage and family therapist. Most of us are only willing to see a doctor when we are ill, or have experienced a physical trauma or crisis. Yet we fail to see any value in consulting a physician for preventive measures. It inevitably costs more to treat than to prevent.

In my practice, couples whose marriages are in crisis will come in for sessions often and pay the fee without hesitation. However, when the crisis has passed and I suggest learning a few skills to ward off further crises and problems, many couples fail to see the value, or express financial inability to support such a preventive measure. However, ". . . prevention works! You and your family can save a lot of pain, worry and money by avoiding health problems in the first place" (Kemper et al., 1995, 17).

Conventional medicine found its limelight in treating acute diseases, addressing major accidents, handling emergency situations and providing life-saving techniques in war time. However, it has been less successful in the treatment of chronic diseases which are the result of the aging process and the lifestyles which we live (Rector-Page, 1992). As we struggle with more chronic diseases, it has forced us to begin to take more responsibility for our own health. As this move toward self-responsibility occurs, there seems to be a renewed interest in prevention, and in natural healing and remedies as a first line of defense when illness occurs. "The best news is that natural remedies work - often far better than current medical prescriptions" (Rector-Page, 1992, p. 8). Maybe the moms who served chicken soup when we were sick and had to stay home from school really knew what they were doing!

WHOLISTIC HEALTH

Another shift is occurring in the field of medicine and health care. More and more, it is being fully understood that we are best treated as a "whole." Doctors are better understanding that the emotional/psychological side of a person has a major impact on health. The clergy is beginning to realize that health concerns affect a person's spirituality. Psychologists are becoming aware that food allergies can affect a person's mood. Airola (1971) summarized this emerging concept well: "New medical thinking is directed toward a concept of a man as a whole entity with his physical and emotional aspects inseparably united in one living soul" (Airola, 1971, 176).

Our mind, bodies, emotions and spirit (or soul) are intricately intertwined and we cannot treat one without affecting the other. "There is a direct connection between the mental state of the patient and the ability of the immune system to do its job. Emotional devastation impairs immune function" (Rector-Page, 1992, p. 8). We know that the healing ability of the body is enhanced if we can hold panic and depression at bay. When we are able to be calm and hopeful (as opposed to panicked and depressed), our body's interleukin production is increased. These interleukins assist our bodies in fighting off infections. The presence of panic causes our blood vessels to constrict, which puts a burden on the heart. And depression is known for intensifying infection and disease in our body and weakening our immune system to the point that it is ineffective in fighting new infection and disease.

Dr. Deepak Chopra has been an outspoken supporter of recognizing the distinct connections between mind, body and spirit. His best-selling book, *Ageless Body, Timeless Mind* addresses these issues: "A bout of depression can wreak havoc with the immune system; falling in love can boost it. Despair and helplessness raise the risk of heart attacks and cancer, thereby shortening life. Joy and fulfillment keep us healthy and extend life. This means that the line between biology and psychology can't really be drawn with any certainty. A remembered stress, which is only a wisp of thought, releases the same flood of destructive hormones as the stress itself" (Chopra, 1993, 5).

As the connections between mind, body, emotions, and spirit are recognized, there seems to be more cooperation between various fields of health care. Recently, one of my clients expressed concern that her husband might not understand some of her health concerns, placing stress on the marriage. In a cooperative effort, her physician, her physical therapist, her children's therapist and me (as the family therapist) all agreed to meet with her and her husband to discuss these issues as they interrelate. This kind of teaming is imperative to address the whole person.

ALTERNATIVE MEDICINE

There was a time when "natural" solutions and alternative medicine were left to the "weird" or to "religious" groups. However, these natural healing methods are now being investigated and honored by renowned doctors, therapists, psychologists, and clergy members. "A growing number of physicians who write health-oriented books are suggesting to their readers and patients to go outside the realm of modern medicine to get safer and less expensive remedies for their individual health problems" (Heinerman, 1988, xiii).

This is not to demean the value of the medical field. However, we all could gain from taking responsibility for our own health, seeking preventive measures, using natural healing measures as a first line of defense, and then consulting our physicians when we do not see improvement, or when we experience crisis/emergency types of health situations. This book is about taking responsibility, employing preventive measures, and embracing natural healing methods and remedies.

2 Phytochemicals: What They Are & What They Do

"In the world where science merges with health, phytochemicals are the next big thing."
—Begley, *Newsweek*

"Since prehistoric time, man has been trying to find more useful plants and to improve the yield and the quality of the known ones" (Verpoorte, 1989, 43). The plant world is so valuable to us, not only because plants provide shade in the summer, produce beautiful flowers for our tables, and supply us with food to eat, but also because they are a vital part of the circle of life. They provide us means of fuel, they are used as building materials, they provide the fibers which made the paper in this book you are holding and the material from which the clothing you have on was made. They provide bulk chemicals (like rubber for tires) and fine chemicals (for pharmaceuticals, flavoring, color dyes, insecticides, antioxidants and pheromones) Verpoorte, 1989.

In our culture, plants were revered for their healing properties more in years past than in recent years. In the third-world, or "developing countries," that reverence has remained through the years. Perhaps that was due to their lack of financial means to obtain both over-the-counter and prescription drugs in the manner we have been afforded. Although for years our scientists, biochemists and researchers seemed to have their focus set on the world of synthetic drugs, the revolution of looking to the healing properties in plants now seems to be recurring in our country.

THE STUDY OF PLANTS

Preserving plant species and continuing to study the benefits of plants is critical. These studies can lead to fine chemicals and pharmaceuticals which could be beneficial to all mankind.

Archaeological studies indicate that there are more than 3,000 species of plants that have been used for food. However, we obtain most proteins and carbohydrates in our diets from only about 30 species, a mere 1/100th of those available to us. Our vegetable consumption comes from about 15 species and our fruit consumption from about 15 other species (Verpoorte, 1989). This leaves many species which are just beginning to be studied so that we can learn more about their phytochemical compounds and their benefits.

The knowledge of plants, their benefits, and how we can protect them from becoming extinct is of paramount importance. Another important aspect of plant studies is learning more about correct preparation and application of plant substances. Processes done incorrectly can nullify active ingredients in plants (Hudson & Towers, 1991).

As stated in Chapter One, those living in "developing countries" are in dire need of less expensive, naturally available treatments and remedies. In 1986, these "developing countries" used $18.5 million of pharmaceuticals, while many other people in need were unable to obtain or afford them. "The health standards of these third-world people even such as they are, have to be sustained by other therapies, and phytopharmaceuticals play a major role in this" (Wijesekera, 1991, 217).

GROWTH IN THE FIELD OF PHYTOCHEMISTRY

All of these factors have led to a phenomenal growth in the field of phytochemistry. Phytochemistry is the field which studies the chemical components of plants. These chemical components sometimes protect the plants from sunlight, but they also have an effect on people, too. Gordon defines a phytochemical as the chemicals found in plants which are not vitamins or minerals, but are "full of health promoting qualities that can supercharge your diet" (Gordon, 1994, p. 32). Crabb (1995) points out that these chemicals have no nutritional value, meaning that the body does not have to have them in order to run efficiently. But she adds that their value is in their ability to fight disease. These phytochemical compounds are considered a blockbuster in the health care field. You can hardly pick up a ladies magazine, a health magazine or a home magazine without finding some information about the phytochemical revolution within their pages. "... [They] have never seen the inside of a vitamin bottle for the simple reason that scientists have not, until very recently, even known they existed, let alone brewed them into pills" (Begley, 1994, 45). These newly hailed phytochemical compounds are in explosive growth.

THE IMPORTANCE OF PHYTOCHEMICALS

Various researchers and writers are hailing the importance with statements such as the following. "Vegetables . . . contain a wide range of chemopreventive compounds that go way beyond vitamins" (Gordon, 1994, 32). "In general it is reasonable to assume that compounds isolated from plants, especially traditional medicinal plants, offer better chances of safe administration than synthetic drugs" (Hudson & Towers., 1991, p. 216). "A whole crop of studies has found that components of such diverse foods as green tea, broccoli, berries, and carrots can actually protect us against heart disease and cancer" (Crabb, 1995, p. 38).

The above statements are only the beginning of the results of studies on phytochemicals. Phytochemicals impact almost every aspect of our health. For example, beta carotene is actually a form of Vitamin A which our bodies can readily use. It is found abundantly in many fruits and vegetables. Recently, research has indicated that it is not only an effective antioxidant, but it reduces the risk of chronic diseases (Ziegler et al., 1992).

Dr. Gordon (1994) in the Journal of Longevity Research wrote a paragraph which gives an indication of the breadth of the benefits of phytochemicals:

"Epidemiologic research at Harbin Medical College in China provides evidence that cabbage reduces stomach cancer risk. Other phytochemicals like gingerol protect against ulcers. Rosemarinic acid stimulates the heart to produce a strong rhythmic beat. Ginkgo biloba promotes circulation to the extremities, prevents blood clots, scavenges free radicals, and may offer protection against Alzheimer's disease. Green tea polyphenols cut down cholesterol much like the drug Questran, reduce blood pressure, fight infectious diseases such as the flu, and even freshen the breath. Hawthorn berry extract fights plaque deposits in the arteries. Spirulina detoxifies the blood. There is a veritable wealth of health benefits in phytochemicals . . ." (Gordon, 1994, p. 34).

A FIVE YEAR STUDY OF PHYTOCHEMICALS

Understanding the great importance of these phytochemicals, the National Cancer Institute launched a multimillion dollar, five year study of them in 1989. The United States Department of Agriculture (USDA) also understands the ben-

efits in phytochemicals. They recommend in their food pyramid for daily intake:
- 3 - 5 servings of vegetables
- 2 - 4 servings of fruits
- 6 - 11 helpings of whole grains.

Although Dr. Gordon (1994) supports these high intakes of fruits, vegetables, and grains, he notes that an adult would have to eat five to ten pounds of food daily to obtain the benefits afforded to us in these foods. Currently, only nine percent of Americans eat enough broccoli to get the maximum health benefits that it has to offer, much less other vegetables and fruits. However, if Americans were to eat by the prescribed food pyramid, it is predicted that the cancer rate in America would decline dramatically (Gordon, 1994).

THE BIOTECHNOLOGICAL INDUSTRY DESIGNS FOODS

The lack of intake of appropriate foods has led to a growth in the biotechnological industry. "Biotechnology in nutritional research and food product development includes increased understanding of the effect of bioactive substances on metabolism and the development of specialized technologies for the production of novel food" (Kitts, 1994, 431). In addition, "applications of biotechnology could result in the production of foods with added potential for therapeutic roles in enhancing health or controlling diet-related chronic diseases such as atherosclerosis and cancer" (Kitts, 1994, 431).

This has led to a new field being called "Designer Foods" by many. The term was formerly the name of one of the programs at the National Cancer Institute. It is no longer called the "Designer Foods Program" but is now called the "Phytochemical Research Component of the Diet in Cancer Research Program." The institute is currently sponsoring research on the disease-fighting capabilities of edible plants such as licorice root, garlic, flaxseed, soybeans, green peas, carrots, lettuce, oranges, apples, and pears (Crabb, 1995).

These "designer foods" are foods which are to be fortified with extracted and stabilized compounds from plants. While I have adopted the National Cancer Institute's name "designer foods," some call them "nutriceuticals" and others call them "performance foods" (Kitts, 1994), "functional foods," "phytochemical sources," and "phytogenic substances" (Hathcock, 1993). Whatever label you put on them, food industries around the world are gearing up to join the creation of these "designer foods" . . . food packed with beneficial doses of phytochemicals. "Unifying efforts of food, nutritional, and medical scientists and dieticians will result in the development of thoroughly evaluated new food products with the potential for contributing to disease prevention and treatment strategies" (Kitts, 1994, p. 431).

DESIGNER FOODS

One example of a "designer food" is the possibility of using licorice root as a sweetener in snacks. It is calorie-free,

Phytochemicals: What They Are & What They Do

50 times sweeter than sugar, and it fights tooth decay, prevents colon cancer, and the Japanese say it slows the progression of HIV into AIDS (Crabb, 1995). Another example of a "designer food" is producing "high octane" orange juice by loading it with phytochemicals that remove lead from the body. This particular "designer food" could target inner city school children who have often shown highly dangerous levels of lead in their blood (Crabb, 1995).

Dr. Herbert Pierson, the former director of the National Cancer Institute's Designer Foods Program is now in Woodville, Washington, as a nutrition consultant. He envisioned that these foods could take the "guesswork" out of determining which food contained which phytochemicals. And it would also remove the concern about how they would have to be prepared (cooked, raw, cold, etc.) in order to preserve their benefits.

While the food industry is attempting to capitalize on "designer foods," the nutritional supplement business is examining methods of flash-freeze-drying these phytochemicals and putting them in pill or capsule form. One of the benefits of flash-freeze-drying them is that this removes all hydration, which also carries out any toxins from pesticides. One company, Mannatech Incorporated, in Grand Prairie, Texas, has actually contracted with the Gummi Bear Company and has put these phytochemicals in naturally sweetened gummi bear form for children.

Regardless of what form we get these phytochemicals

in, whether it be in capsule form, gummi bear form, "designer food" form, or mass consumption of vegetables, fruits, and grains, there are tremendous health benefits, both in the realm of prevention and the realm of treatment. This book will attempt to explore those benefits.

"We anticipate that, on the basis of historical experience with the many pharmacologically useful compounds that have been obtained from plants, as well as experimental tests, there are probably innumerable potentially useful antiviral, antimicrobial, antiparasitic, and anti-insecticidal phytochemicals awaiting characterization" (Hudson & Towers, 1991, p. 182).

3 Fruits & Vegetables

"Nutrition experts have tirelessly pointed out that the evidence is much stronger for a diet rich in fruits and vegetables than for any individual nutrients."
—*Consumer Reports on Health,* April, 1995

The Surgeon General Report on Health and Nutrition (1988) linked nutritional problems to five of the ten leading causes of death in the United States (heart disease, cancer, strokes, non-insulin dependent diabetes mellitus, and arteriosclerosis). This admonishes us to take a serious look at what we eat and how it affects our health.

Few of us eat to preserve our health or to nourish ourselves. Perhaps the two primary selection criteria of what we eat are our cravings and the convenience with which we can get the food. Think honestly about it. How long has it been since you thought: "What do I need to eat for dinner?" No! We normally call our spouses, significant others, friends, family members and say, "What would you like to eat for dinner?"

And perhaps far too often our response is: "Let's just drive through Taco Bell or What-A-Burger on the way to the mall" or "Let's just grab a hot dog when we get to the game." Of course, there is nothing wrong with a salad at Taco Bell, or a chicken sandwich at What-A-Burger (and surely there is some nutritional saving grace about a hot dog at the ball game!), but certainly, we fail to consider what our bodies need for health in most of our considerations about eating.

In fact, our consistent failure to consume the foods we need is quite astonishing. In 1990, a study was done to determine how many fruits and vegetables Americans consumed. It is astounding to note that the study indicated that 45 percent of Americans polled had consumed no fruits or fruit juice that day, and 22 percent had consumed no vegetables (Blossom et al., 1990). Only 20 percent of Americans eat five servings of fruits and vegetables daily, and only five percent eat seven or more servings (*Consumer Reports on Health*, January, 1993).

Add to our poor consumption of nutritious foods the fact that 58.1 percent of Americans report little or no physical exercise (American Journal of Nursing, 1994), and it is absolutely no wonder that at least 26 percent of American adults are obese (*Healthy People 2000*, 1990). "Research clearly shows that a diet with plenty of fruits and vegetables is good for health, but Americans are not reaching the basic goal of five or more servings each day" (Yen, 1992).

DO WE EAT AS WE SHOULD FOR THE SAKE OF OUR HEALTH?

As mentioned earlier, the Food Guide Pyramid issued by the United States Department of Agriculture (1992) recommends three to five servings of vegetables daily, two to four of fruit, and six to eleven of grains. That would be a minimum of five servings of fruits and vegetables daily. And 80 percent of us do not do it!

Is it that we, as a nation, have tremendous amounts of knowledge and information available to us about our health and how to promote our health, yet we refuse to practice responsible health care? I have a friend who has high blood pressure (for which he takes medication) and is a very intelligent man. He knows the importance of diet and exercise in the treatment of his blood pressure. Yet, he continues to eat eggs, sausage and hash browns for breakfast, and reads in his leisure time instead of exercising. I admonished him about his eating and lack of exercise recently and told him that if he really cared about his kids, loved ones and friends, he would take care of himself. I found out from another mutual friend that at breakfast the following morning he ordered a "light omelet" made of egg whites only and had taken a walk the night before. He, of course, announced at breakfast that he had been "chewed out." Perhaps as a nation, we all need a good "chewing out" if that's what will make us more aware of our health and will cause us to take responsibility for it.

EATING SENSIBLY FOR THE SAKE OF OUR HEALTH

Eating fruits and vegetables makes sense!. . . even if there were no phytochemical benefits. "Increasing the consumption of complex carbohydrates in the form of fruit and vegetables can displace consumption of fats and hence reduce total caloric intake and improve health status, (Neill & Allensworth, 1994, p. 150). Additionally, both fruits and vegetables contain little to no fat and are high in fiber. For example, one cup of cooked legumes contains five grams of fiber and less than one gram of fat (*Mayo Clinic Health Letter*, 1992).

The most commonly purchased fruits in America are apples, oranges and bananas (Yen, 1992). The reason for that may be the ease in preparation of these fruits, along with their year-round availability. The most commonly purchased vegetables are lettuce, tomatoes, carrots, and celery (Yen, 1992). These are common ingredients in salads, as well as sandwich fillers.

Fruits & Vegetables

THE 5-A-DAY PROGRAM

Being aware of the lack of consumption of the necessary fruits and vegetables, the National Cancer Institute launched a 5-A-Day program to increase awareness about their value and to increase American consumption of them (Neill & Allensworth, 1994). Studies indicate that older Americans are slightly more conscious and compliant with consuming fruits and vegetables on a daily basis than are younger Americans (Yen, 1992). Reasons named for the lack of consumption of fruits and vegetables are: they are inconvenient, most must be prepared (peeled, washed, cooked, etc.) and grabbing a bag of chips is easier; they can cause flatulence (gas); and they are more expensive than a candy bar or french fries (Yen, 1992).

DIETS OF AMERICAN KIDS AND TEENS

In a survey conducted among 3,112 kids in grades two through six, it was found that 24 percent had eaten no fruits the day before and 24.9 had eaten no vegetables the day before (Friend, 1995). That means that one-fourth of those children consumed absolutely no fruits or vegetables. In an article published in *USA Today* on March 29, 1995, Dr. Ernst Wynder of the American Health Foundation in New York was quoted as saying: "That finding suggests problems ahead for many children, since 35 percent of all cancer is attributed to diet."

In another survey, the Youth Risk Behavior Surveillance System interviewed high school students, grades nine through twelve. The results indicated that only 10 percent of the female students and 15 percent of the male students consumed five or more servings of fruits and vegetables daily (Centers for Disease Control, 1991).

For years it has been noted that the school might be able to play a role in the health and nutrition of students. In 1946, Congress passed the National School Lunch Act in order to help in the promotion of the health of school children by offering low-cost nutritious lunches (Neill & Allensworth., 1994). This would seem an ideal avenue since the National Adolescent Student Health Survey noted that 75 percent of the kids who ate their lunch at school bought their meals at the school cafeteria (Burghart & Devany, 1993). But a dismaying fact is that an assessment study of nutrition and diet in schools found that cafeteria meals served in schools contain 38 percent fat (Burghart & Devany, 1993).

The National Adolescent Student Health Survey (1989) noted that most teenagers are aware that a diet high in fat, sugar and salt is not good for their health. However, half of those surveyed indicated that they ate three or more snacks daily that were essentially empty calories (high in fat, sugar and salt).

EDUCATING KIDS, TEENS AND THEIR PARENTS

In an attempt to address such poor eating, the American Cancer Society (1993) has attempted to educate both kids and their parents. They set their goals as being: 1) to increase the numbers of students eating five or more servings of fruits and vegetables daily to 35 percent; and 2) to get at least 80 percent of those same students to limit their intake of high fat snacks to less than two daily.

In a study involving fourth and fifth graders, three ways to increase fruit and vegetable intake were identified. One was to have parents make fruits and vegetables readily available at home. The second was to assist in cultivating a taste for them. The final way to increase their consumption was to teach them the skills necessary to prepare fruits and vegetables (Baranowski et al., 1993). One writer went a step further, stating that having children grow their own fruits and vegetables might be a sure way to increase their consumption. "Nobody can resist tasting something they've labored over" (Sanders, 1982, 19).

Whatever method is used to get children to increase their consumption of fruits and vegetables, one thing is certain . . . parents play a significant role in the process. Parents should be role models for children. If we eat (and enjoy eating) lots of fruits and vegetables, our kids will likely do the same. It is also the parent who buys the food and places it in the home. If there are "Twinkies" in a bowl on the table, we certainly can't expect a child to go search through the crisper in the refrigerator for an apple.

As adults, we must take responsibility for our health and well-being. That means eating nutritiously (with at least five servings of fruits and vegetables daily), getting sufficient rest and exercising regularly. And if we model this for our children, the next generation might surprise us with their improved health.

4 Phytochemicals in Fruits & Vegetables

"Phytochemicals are strong candidates for extending the best years of life."
—Dr. Jay Gordon, 1994

Phytochemicals are present in all fruits and vegetables, and there are probably many more than those we know about currently. For example, a tomato may contain as many as 10,000 phytochemicals (Crabb, 1995). However, a tomato grown in Texas and a tomato grown in California may not contain the exact same phytochemicals.

However, there are some phytochemicals found consistently in some fruits and vegetables. This chapter will cover some of those fruits and vegetables, the phytochemicals they contain and the potential benefits to be gained from them.

TOMATOES

Tomatoes (*Lycopersicon esculentum*) are the most often consumed "fruit or vegetable" in the United States (Heinerman, 1988). "Fruit or vegetable" is in quotes because whether a tomato is a fruit or vegetable has been an age-old discussion. Botanically, a tomato is a fruit. However, in 1893, it took a Supreme Court ruling to declare it a vegetable (Heinerman, 1988).

Whether you consider tomatoes a fruit or a vegetable, there are many known benefits from eating them. In Japan, it was found that fresh tomato juice accelerated blood sugar formation in rabbits by liver stimulation. In the Soviet Union, tomatoes are consumed by factory workers to detoxify their bodies of chemicals to which they are exposed as part of their work. The chlorine and sulfur in the tomatoes helps the liver filter the toxins, remove them from the system and protect the liver from cirrhosis (Heinerman, 1988).

Tomatoes are also rich in carotenoids. As a matter of fact, they have been called the richest source of carotenoids. One of the carotenoids in tomatoes is lycopene. It is one of the most effective scavengers of free radicals. (Read more about free radicals and their impact on the body in Chapter 13.) Another carotenoid found in tomatoes is canthaxanthin. In 1991, an article published in Oncology noted that in studies using rodents, canthaxanthin was shown to prevent breast cancer (Gordon, 1994). In addition, tomatoes contain coumarins, which have been shown to have anticancer properties and may prevent blood clots (Hermann, 1994). Research has specifically linked tomatoes to prevention of pancreatic and cervical cancer (Carper, 1993). A study conducted at Johns Hopkins University indicated that low levels of lycopene in the blood is a predictor of pancreatic cancer (Carper, 1993). Therefore, tomatoes, which are rich in lycopene, are critically important to those at risk for pancreatic cancer.

A study conducted at the Cancer Research Center at the University of Hawaii noted that all vegetables, including tomatoes, dramatically reduced the risk of lung cancer. Women who ate these vegetables doubled their expected survival time and men extended their expected survival times as well (Carper, 1993).

When we have eaten too much fat, tomatoes may prove very helpful. When eating fatty foods like butter, fried foods and meat with fat, tomatoes may actually help dissolve the fat, which could prevent arteriosclerosis.

HOT PEPPERS

Hot peppers, such as cayenne, contain capsaicin. Capsaicin may actually stop the development of some types of cancer by preventing toxic substances from attaching themselves into the DNA of the cells in our bodies (Hermann, 1994).

It may seem surprising, but the phytochemical compounds in hot peppers actually help in protecting the stomach's lining. One study in Austria indicated that aspirin, known to damage the stomach's lining, was given to experimental animals. The aspirin caused tissue damage to the stomach's lining as was expected. However, another set of experimental animals was given aspirin, along with capsaicin from hot peppers. Those animals given the hot peppers with the aspirin had 92 percent less bleeding in their stomach linings (Carper, 1993).

Capsaicin is the substance in the hot pepper that produces burning in the mouth. That chemical is very similar to guaifensein, an expectorant found in three-fourths of cough medicines. Therefore, hot peppers have been shown effective in the treatment of colds, flu, bronchitis, sinusitis and hay fever.

Another interesting benefit of the phytochemicals in hot peppers is their ability to give us an uplift in our mood. These phytochemicals can actually create the release of endorphins from the brain, which causes a "natural rush."

CARROTS

Carrots contain carotenoids, which are also found in tomatoes. They may prevent lung cancer by protecting the cells in our bodies from various toxins (Hermann, 1994). Carotenoids can reduce the risk of heart disease by at least one-half according to the American Heart Association (Jack, 1991).

In a study following almost 2,000 men for a period of

nineteen years, it was found that those who consumed carrots on a regular basis had significantly less incidence of lung cancer (Shekelle et al., 1981).

Carotenoids found in carrots can also stimulate the human immune response, increasing T-helper cell numbers (Prabhala, 1990). This is of particular interest to scientists studying the dietary role in treating AIDS patients.

Carrots eaten regularly by women cut the rate of strokes by 68 percent (Carper, 1993). They have also proven effective in lowering blood cholesterol levels, reducing the risk of cataracts and promoting regularity (Carper, 1993).

CRUCIFEROUS VEGETABLES:
(BROCCOLI, BRUSSELS SPROUTS, CABBAGE, KALE, TURNIPS, CAULIFLOWER AND TURNIP GREENS)

The cruciferous vegetable family (genus *Brassica*) has been shown to have chemopreventive factors in carcinogenicity in studies using laboratory animals (Haenzel et al., 1980; Whitty & Bjeldanes, 1987). Any studies indicating prevention or treatment for cancer should get our immediate and undivided attention. And this vegetable family, the cruciferous vegetables, has been studied extensively in this arena.

For example, broccoli, kale, Brussels sprouts, and cabbage all contain indole-3-carbinol. This chemical substance regulates the manner and speed at which the body metabolizes estrogen and other hormones. These are the hormones which studies have indicated might cause cancer of the reproductive system, breast cancer and prostate cancer. Our body can turn these hormones into toxic compounds which do damage to our cells, leading to improper growth and division, which can be the beginning of cancer. Indole-3-carbinol not only has the capacity to serve as a preventive in that process, but it also promotes the production of benign estrogen and other benign hormones in our bodies (Gordon, 1994). Another benefit of indole-3-carbinol is that it makes it easier for the body to expel and excrete toxins that could cause a variety of cancers.

There has been extensive focus on the phytochemical components in broccoli. It contains sulforaphane, a compound which activates anticancer enzymes. These enzymes remove chemicals from the cells that might cause cancer. Broccoli also contains phenethyl isothiocyanate. This chemical compound stops the activity of enzymes (that could stimulate our genes to develop cancer) from binding to the genetic coding in our cells, which would result in the spreading of cancer (Gordon, 1994). In addition, broccoli contains chlorophyll, which blocks chemicals that could cause degenerative diseases, including cancer from genetic mutation (Gordon, 1994). It also contains lutein, an antioxidant that some researchers believe to be as powerful a cancer preventive as beta carotene (Carper, 1993).

In a study involving over two hundred females, the importance of eating cruciferous vegetables by lung cancer patients was remarkably underlined. The study indicated that those who ate lots of cruciferous vegetables, especially broccoli, had a survival rate of thirty-three months, compared to eighteen months in those who ate little or none (Carper, 1993).

The folic acid in broccoli can "stop the virus that can lead to cervical cancer" (Carper, 1993, 265.) In a study at the University of Alabama at Birmingham, it was found that women infected with the virus that can lead to cervical cancer had significantly lower levels of folic acid than those who had the virus, but did not develop cervical cancer (Carper, 1993).

Broccoli is also a rich source of chromium. Chromium is a trace mineral that tends to regulate blood sugar, an important consideration for those with diabetes or those with a family history of diabetes. Chromium can prevent diabetes or normalize borderline sugar levels, whether they are high or low. For those diabetics on insulin treatment, chromium tends to increase the efficiency of insulin (Carper, 1993).

Another member of the cruciferous vegetable family is cabbage. Cabbage has been shown to suppress the growth of polyps, which can be a prelude to colon cancer. Studies have indicated that men eating cabbage more often than once per week cut their chance of contracting colon cancer 66 percent (Carper, 1993). The juice from cabbage has also been shown to relieve the discomfort from stomach ulcers and, in some cases, actually heal them.

Cabbage also contains phytochemicals with interesting topical benefits. "Babe Ruth wore cabbage leaves under his baseball cap to keep his head cool" (Corrieri, 1992, 126). On a more serious note, cool green cabbage compresses have anti-inflammatory, anti-edema and anti-infectious properties. Breast feeding mothers with engorgement have found that cool cabbage compresses, followed by hot compresses and a massage facilitates the flow of milk (Corrier, 1992).

Kale, broccoli, and greens are an excellent bioavailable source of calcium for women. This is especially important in considering osteoporosis. In a study done at Creighton and Purdue Universities, it was found that women absorbed more calcium from kale than from milk (Heaney and Weaver 1990).

The cruciferous vegetables are most effective as anticancer agents if eaten raw. Cooking them tends to destroy the indoles, which renders their antiestrogen and anticancer properties ineffective.

There are obviously major benefits to be gained from increasing our intake of cruciferous vegetables. No matter how much we ingest, they certainly will not harm us. Experiments have shown that there was no toxicity when there was a high intake of cruciferous vegetables (Clandinin and Robblee, 1981).

CITRUS FRUITS: ORANGES, LEMONS AND GRAPEFRUITS

Oranges and other citrus fruits, such as grapefruit, tangerines and lemons, contain limonoids. These chemical compounds are of critical importance in the body because they break down many chemicals, which, if left in the body, could cause cancer (Hermann, 1994). Oranges contain carotenoids, terpenes, flavonoids, vitamin C, coumarins, glucarate and beta carotene, which are all natural cancer preventives. One study found "that citrus fruits possess fifty-eight known anticancer chemicals, more than any other food" (Carper, 1993, 210).

Oranges are also a source for glutathione, which is an antioxidant. Low levels of this antioxidant are found in the lenses of the eyes of people with cataracts (Carper, 1993).

The pulp of grapefruit contains a unique pectin that has been shown to lower cholesterol and reverse atherosclerosis in animal studies. It has also been shown to be extremely effective in the prevention of stomach and pancreatic cancer (Carper, 1993).

PAPAYAS

The carpain in papaya is a phytochemical which has proven to be very valuable in treating the heart. Rex Adams (1977), a Medical Research Reporter, revealed a case study regarding the condition of a 30-year-old woman who had experienced multiple cardiovascular angina attacks. After taking massive amounts of medication which seemed not to help her condition, someone advised that she eat only mangoes and papayas. Shortly, her heart returned to normal, pain free.

RASPBERRIES, GRAPES, STRAWBERRIES AND BLUEBERRIES

These fruits all contain phenols. Phenols have the capacity to trap toxic chemicals in the body and flush them out. This may reduce the risk of cancer (Hermann, 1994).

The Swedish botanist Linnaeus reported that strawberries, eaten in large quantities twice daily, cured gout (Salaman and Scheer, 1994). Strawberries have also been shown to be a bodyguard of cholesterol levels, assisting in raising HDL levels, and lowering LDL levels (Carper, 1993).

Grapes contain boron, an element noted for improving brainpower. Increased intake of boron can stimulate mental alertness, reduce drowsiness and improve mental performance. Boron has also been shown to be a type of mild estrogen replacement therapy, a very important consideration with osteoporosis (Carper, 1993). Because of its estrogen-like properties, boron has also been effective in treating the symptoms associated with menopause.

Red grapes contain quercetin, an antioxidant. Quercetin, in laboratory tests, also proved to be antibacterial and antiviral (Carper, 1993).

Raspberries have been called the "natural aspirin" because they contain many aspirin-like compounds. Blueberries have these same aspirin-like qualities.

Blueberries are rich in anthocyanosides, chemicals which kill bacteria. Because of this antibacterial property, they have long been used in Sweden to treat childhood diarrhea.

Because they are effective in fighting E. coli, the bacteria that is associated with urinary tract and bladder infections, they have been used to treat both of those infections (Carper, 1993). These anthocyanoside compounds have been shown to effectively slow down visual losses, particularly those associated with aging.

Berries are also rich in ellagic acid. These are important because they prevent toxic chemicals that can damage cells from being activated (Crabb, 1995).

APPLES

Some people believe that the "forbidden fruit" in the Garden of Eden was the apple. Some people believe that it was an apple tree that George Washington cut down when he "could not tell a lie." But whether or not either of these stories really involved apples, we do know that early ancient history recorded the use of apples. Throughout the world, there are more than 1400 varieties of apples (Hermann, 1994). Apples have a long history of physical benefit. In July, 1978, the *American Journal of Clinical Nutrition* noted that apples served as a laxative by increasing bulk and decreasing the time between bowel movements.

Apples serve as an infection fighter, much like penicillin. They also decrease tooth decay when eaten often as snacks.

According to a study conducted at the University of Texas Health Science Center in San Antonio, colon cancer in laboratory animals was reduced by 50 percent when they were fed pectin from apples (Carper, 1993). In addition, their cholesterol levels dropped by about 30 percent.

Another study conducted by French researchers confirmed that pectin found in apples is effective in lowering LDL cholesterol levels. In their study, men and women were given two to three apples daily for a month. By the end of the month, 80 percent of them had lower cholesterol levels (Sable-Amplis, 1983).

Apples also contain salicylates. Aspirin has been studied and found to be a deterrent to colon cancer (Carper, 1993). The salicylates in apples have the same qualities as aspirin and are being investigated for their effectiveness in fighting and preventing colon cancer.

Another phytochemical found in apples is glucarates. They help the body get rid of some of the steroidal hormones, which have been linked to breast and prostate cancers (Crabb, 1995).

ARTICHOKES

Artichokes, like apples, are known to have cholesterol-reducing properties. They contain cynarin, which protects from atherosclerosis and from hardening of the arteries. Artichokes have been known to have an activating effect in the brain and the central nervous system. In addition, the acids in artichokes help to improve liver function (Heinerman, 1988).

ONIONS

Onions may be one of the most controversial vegetables. While some enjoy their taste and use them in many foods, others, particularly lovers, more often than not say "Cut or hold the onions." Although quite flavorful, the odor they leave on the eater's breath seems to go on and on and on, much like the Energizer Bunny that never runs down. Peeling and cutting them up not only brings tears to the eyes of the cook, but the odor can also linger on the hands after many washings. Looking past the odor that onions leave behind provides some interesting health information.

The onion (as well as garlic) is one of the oldest medicines prescribed. "It's an ancient truth: garlic and onions are strong medicines against unwanted blood clots. An early Egyptian papyrus called onions a tonic for the blood. Early American doctors prescribed onions as 'blood purifiers.' French farmers fed horses garlic and onions to dissolve blood clots in their legs" (Carper, 1993, 72).

Onions contain adenosine, which is a natural muscle relaxer, according to studies out of George Washington University (Carper, 1993). Onions also contain prostaglandin Al and E, both having the effect of lowering blood pressure.

A study from India demonstrated that onions are a superb fat blocker! In the study, men were fed a meal very high in fat. Their blood tests following the meal indicated that the clot-dissolving activity plunged dramatically. However, when fed the same high-fat meal with two ounces of onion added, their blood tests had indicated that the onions totally reversed the fat's detrimental effects on the dissolving of clots (Carper, 1983).

The quercetin, found in yellow and red onions, is a mild sedative. When ingested by laboratory animals, their central nervous system was affected, followed by drowsiness (Carper, 1993). Therefore, onions have proven effective in treating anxiety and some sleep disorders.

Onions also contain diallyl sulfide and ajoene. These two compounds, along with the quercetin, block nitrosamines and aflatoxin, some of the most powerful cancer-causing agents, particularly known for causing stomach, lung and liver cancer. One study from China, sponsored by the National Cancer Institute, highlighted the preventive benefits of onions on stomach cancer. In the study, those who consumed three ounces of onions daily had a 60 percent lower chance of developing stomach cancer (Carper, 1993).

Onions have also been noted as an anti-skin cancer agent. The quercetin seems to provide protection from melanoma (Carper, 1993).

A study from Harvard Medical School has noted the effectiveness of onions in raising HDL cholesterol levels (the "good guy" cholesterol). It was found that half a raw onion raises HDL levels about 30 percent in people with heart disease (Carper, 1993).

In Europe and Middle Eastern countries, onions have long been used as a treatment for diabetics. Researchers from India found that the more onions given to patients, the more the blood sugar levels were depressed (Carper, 1993). Allyl propyl disulfide and allicin are the compounds believed to be anti-diabetic in the onion. These compounds are similar to tolbutamide, a pharmaceutical used to stimulate insulin synthesis and release. In a study with laboratory animals, it was found that the compounds from onions were 77 percent as effective as the pharmaceuticals administered to the diabetic animals (Carper, 1993).

Onions are superior anti-inflammatories, often used to treat colds, asthma and bronchitis. Diphenylthiosulfinate, one compound in onions, was studied for its anti-inflammatory properties. It was found that it had anti-inflammatory activity superior to that of prednisone, a popular anti-inflammatory pharmaceutical. When given to laboratory animals, diphenylthiosulfinate reduced the risk of asthma attacks. In studies with humans, the compound reduced bronchial asthma attacks by 50 percent (Carper, 1993). The quercetin compound, mentioned earlier, was also shown to relieve allergies and hay fever. The compounds were effective by dilating air passages, thinning the mucus in the lungs and reducing inflammation in the air passages.

This is certainly not a comprehensive list of the phytochemicals found in fruits and vegetables. A separate chapter is devoted to garlic because of the massive amounts of studies which report the benefits of its phytochemicals. There are many other fruits and vegetables with beneficial phytochem-

The Facts About Phytochemicals

icals, and as studies continue, many more will be identified. Certainly this data should support us in increasing the intake of our fruits and vegetables or of those natural phytochemical supplements available to us.

Garlic: The Miracle Plant

"Modern research has confirmed that garlic and onions do indeed possess miracle healing powers."
— Airola, 1993

In some people's minds, the only use for garlic is to make excellent bread to go along with their spaghetti. However, garlic may be one of the most useful vegetables known. It has been referred to as the "king of the vegetable kingdom" (Airola, 1991).

Garlic, *Allium sativum*, is a bulbous perennial plant in the lily family. It contains more than 200 beneficial compounds (*Better Nutrition for Today's Living*, 1995). Its high concentrations of volatile oil, mucilage and germanium make it a great remedy for many ailments (Gladstar, 1993). It is also rich in selenium, a heart disease preventive (*Healthy Cell News*, 1995).

HISTORICAL USES OF GARLIC

"Garlic has enjoyed great fame and popularity as a 'miracle, cure-all' clove" (Cawood et al., 1995, 265). As early as 3,000 B.C., the Babylonians were using garlic to cure many diseases (Airola, 1991). Through the ages, many cultures have used garlic to treat a variety of diseases and ailments, such as intestinal disorders, symptoms of premature aging, high or low blood pressure, common colds, intestinal worms, coughs, asthma, whooping cough, dysentery, gas, tuberculosis, diabetes, and as a preventive for tumor formation, diphtheria, typhus, pneumonia, and as an antibiotic (Airola, 1991). Other noted benefits of garlic are that it helps keep weight down, encourages the secretion of hormones, prevents fatigue and promotes the building up of energy (*Healthy Cell News*, 1995).

"Garlic has been used by healers for over 5,000 years of recorded history. Ancient Vikings and Phoenicians never set sail without an abundant supply on board - and probably avoided coming down with scurvy because of it. Early Chinese, Greeks and Romans used garlic to expel intestinal worms, a common and dangerous complaint of the times; to relieve indigestion; to heal skin rashes; to treat respiratory problems; and to stop infection in its tracks. In addition, garlic was and still is thought by many to slow the aging process" (*Healthy Cell News*, 1995).

Garlic: The Miracle Plant

Today, it is not only grandmothers who believe in the miraculous powers of garlic. Even scientists are giving garlic attention as new research shows some remarkable benefits with garlic.

PHYTOCHEMICALS IN GARLIC

The allicin in garlic has antibacterial properties, antiseptic properties, antifungal properties and bacteriostatic properties. Another phytochemical found in garlic is ajoene. This compound, along with adenosine, has been shown to have anti-thrombotic (anti-blood clotting) properties that exceed those of aspirin. Aspirin prevents blood clots by stifling production of thromboxane. The ajoene in garlic also stifles that production, but in addition, it has been shown to block platelet clumping in seven other ways (Carper, 1993). Together, these compounds not only prevent blood clotting, but they also speed up the body's blood clot dissolving activities. These anti-clotting agents can help prevent heart attacks and strokes (*Healthy Cell News*, 1995).

GARLIC AND ARTHRITIS

Some of the compounds in garlic are apparently effective in relieving the pain of osteoarthritis. Researchers in India discovered this accidentally while studying the use of garlic by those with heart disease. They noticed that those patients with joint pain experienced relief by eating two to three garlic gloves daily (Carper, 1993).

GARLIC AND BLOOD PRESSURE

Ingesting garlic seems to have a cumulative effect on lowering blood pressure when consumed on a daily basis (Mowrey, 1986). In an experiment conducted by German researchers, one group had an average blood pressure of 171/102. After three months of being given pills that contained the equivalent of two cloves of garlic daily, the average blood pressure was 152/89 (*Pharmacotherapy*, 1993). The control group, who were given placebos, had no change in blood pressure. The adenosine in garlic is a smooth-muscle relaxant, which allows the muscles in the wall of the blood vessels to dilate, therefore lowering blood pressure. The methyl allyl trisulfide in garlic also expands the walls of the blood vessels (Korotkov, 1966).

GARLIC AND THE NURSING MOTHER

The phytochemicals found in garlic have been reported to do many other interesting things. In a study conducted at the Monnel Chemical Senses Center in Pennsylvania, it was found that infants whose nursing mothers ate garlic or took supplemental garlic, sucked more and drank more milk. Mothers in the control group, who consumed no garlic, found that their babies sucked less and drank less milk (Carper, 1993).

GARLIC AND CANCER

More than 30 anticarcinogens have been identified in the phytochemicals in garlic. Three of those, diallyl sulfide, quercetin and ajoene, have consistently been shown to block cancer in animals in laboratory studies. In a study conducted at M.D. Anderson Cancer Center in Houston, Texas, it was found that mice given garlic, followed by carcinogens had a 75 percent lower rate of contracting colon tumors than those who were given no garlic. In a similar experiment with esophageal cancer, not one animal given garlic developed the cancer (Carper, 1993).

In similar experiments at Pennsylvania State University, the garlic supplement produced a 70 percent lower rate of breast cancer when compared to those given no garlic (Carper, 1993). In a recent edition of the *American Institute for Cancer Research* Newsletter (1995), a report was done regarding those experiments being conducted at Pennsylvania Sate University. The article explained that "garlic may suppress tumor development in two ways: by inhibiting the metabolism of carcinogens in the body and by stopping them from binding to the genetic material" (*American Institute for Cancer Research* Newsletter, 1995, p. 10).

To further the reports of garlic's benefit in relation to cancer, a German study actually found garlic able to destroy malignant human cells, much in the way chemotherapy does. The ajoene in garlic seems to be a "biological response modifier," much like interleukin. The sulfur compounds in garlic have been shown to boost the activity of the macrophages and T-lymphocytes, those parts of our immune system which are called forth to fight when there are malignant cells present in the body (Carper, 1993). Dr. Milner, at Pennsylvania State University's Department of Nutrition is currently conducting clinical trials with human patients to determine how much garlic is needed to be useful in fighting against liver and lung cancer (*American Institute for Cancer Research Newsletter*, 1995).

GARLIC'S EFFECT ON STOMACH AND COLON CANCER

Additionally, these sulfur compounds have been found to fight colon and stomach cancer by acting as an antibiotic. The *H. pylori* bacteria thought to contribute to colon and stomach cancer may be destroyed by the sulfur compounds in garlic.

GARLIC AS AN ANTIBACTERIAL

The antibacterial properties also have proven effective in fighting such bacteria as *Staphylococcus* (which causes abscesses on skin, throat and/or other organs, which can be mild to life-threatening), *Streptococcus* (which causes infections which can attack any organ of the body, found most commonly in the throat), *Brucella* (which causes gastrointestinal difficulties when drinking the milk of infected cows), *Bacillus Vibrio* (which is contracted from eating uncooked or undercooked shellfish and which causes vomiting, abdominal pain and diarrhea), *Klebsiella* (which causes respiratory diseases such as bronchitis, sinusitis and pneumonia), *Proteus* (which causes urinary tract infections, wound infections and diarrhea), *Escherichia* (which is the dreaded infection caused by consuming undercooked meat, which can be deadly), *Salmonella* (which causes gastroenteritis and typhoid fever), *Hafnia, Aeromonas, Citrobacter* and *Providencia* (Cavallito et al., 1945; Huddleson et al., 1944; Jezowa et al., 1966; Johnson and Vaughn, 1969; Sharma et al., 1977).

GARLIC AND PARASITES

The allyl sulfide in garlic has been used in many cultures to kill and expel parasites and worms. The allicin and allyl sulfide have been shown to be effective in treatment of roundworms, pinworms, tapeworms, and hookworms (Stoll & Seebeck, 1951; Jezowa et al., 1966; Yamada and Azuma, 1977).

GARLIC AND CHOLESTEROL LEVELS

At least 20 scientific studies have found that garlic is effective in the reduction of cholesterol (Augusti and Mathew, 1973; Bordia, 1981; Bordia and Bansal, 1973; Bordia et al., 1975; Bordia et al., 1977; Jain, 1975; Jain, 1976; Jain and Konar, 1976; Kamanna and Chandrasekhara, 1982; Kritchevsky, 1975; Petkov, 1979; Sainani et al., 1976). At least six of the many phytochemical compounds in garlic suppress the liver's synthesis of cholesterol, which naturally lowers cholesterol levels. It is believed that the equivalent of three fresh cloves of garlic daily can lower one's cholesterol ten to fifteen percent (Salaman and Scheer, 1994).

Another recent study involving 325 people with elevated cholesterol levels discovered that one-half to one clove of garlic daily lowered their cholesterol levels by about nine percent (*Consumer Reports on Health*, "Overview," 1995). In addition, one study conducted in Seattle at Bastyr College reported that not only were LDL cholesterol levels lowered when garlic was consumed, but that HDL levels were raised 23 percent (Carper, 1993).

GARLIC AS AN ANTIFLATULENT

Another interesting benefit to the phytochemicals contained in garlic is that of an antiflatulent (gas blocker). When beans and other foods known to produce gas are cooked with garlic added, the gas-producing properties are blocked.

GARLIC AND HEART DISEASE

The 15 antioxidant phytochemicals in garlic are particularly significant when considering heart disease. Studies have indicated that garlic consumption not only can prevent artery-clogging, but it even appears to reverse the damage, actually healing previously damaged and clogged arteries.

Dr. Arun Bordia, a pioneer in garlic research, conducted some landmark research on heart patients recovering from heart attacks. He found that those patients consuming two to three cloves of garlic daily had significant benefits when compared to those patients taking no garlic. In the second year, deaths among those patients consuming garlic dropped 50 percent, and in the third year, deaths dropped 66 percent. The group consuming garlic also reported less incidence of chest pain, angina (Carper, 1993).

GARLIC AND THE IMMUNE SYSTEM

As mentioned earlier, the phytochemicals in garlic are very effective in stimulating our immune systems. It has been called by many "the natural antibiotic." The results of one study indicate that one milligram of the allicin in garlic is thought to be equal to 15 standard units of penicillin (Cavallito and Bailey, 1945).

GARLIC AND AIDS

One part of the medical community seriously considering the antibiotic benefits of these phytochemicals is the physicians and health care professionals involved in treating AIDS patients. Some of the opportunitistic or secondary infections that occur in AIDS patients are the result of a weakened or depressed immune system. In the 1920's and 1930's, garlic was used to treat tuberculosis and other lung infections. Therefore, some physicians and researchers are now interested in further investigation regarding the use of the phytochemicals in garlic as an antibiotic in treating AIDS patients.

GARLIC AS AN ANTIBIOTIC

Similarly, garlic has proven effective in treating intestinal parasites, much like an antibiotic. The parasite that is most commonly picked up in drinking water is *Giardia Lamblia*. The normal mode of treatment is antibiotic drugs, normally for ten days. Doctors in Cairo, at the Ain Shams University, found that fresh garlic or supplemental garlic, given to children with this intestinal parasite, wiped out all symptoms in one day (Carper, 1993).

USING GARLIC WITH COLDS AND FLU

It may once have been thought that garlic's ability to fight off colds and flu was just an old wives' tale. However, research from Brigham Young University in Utah has proclaimed that the phytochemical compounds in garlic actually can kill the viruses that are responsible for the development of colds and influenza. Researchers in Rumania and Japan have both independently found the phytochemicals in garlic to be a preventive of the influenza virus (Nagai, 1973).

GARLIC AND YEAST INFECTIONS

The phytochemicals in garlic also have antifungal properties. One of the most significant studies regarding its antifungal properties concerns *Candida Albicans*, the organism responsible for most cases of vaginal yeast infections. Garlic relieved the symptoms of the infection in a majority of the cases studied (Barona and Tansey, 1977). In a book written about natural healing for women, one of the recommendations was to make a suppository of garlic, wrapped in gauze, to treat vaginal yeast infections (Gladstar, 1993).

GARLIC'S ANTIMICROBIAL PROPERTIES

One study in China investigated the effectiveness of the antimicrobial properties in garlic. It focused on the fatal cryptococcal meningitis. In the study, eleven patients were given garlic orally along with intravenous or intramuscular injections. All symptoms were abated, and the patients successfully recovered (Hunan Medical College, 1980).

GARLIC AS AN ANTIDEPRESSANT

Another marvel of the phytochemicals in garlic is their ability to act as a mood elevator. At the University of Hanover in Germany, this was surprisingly substantiated in a study attempting to measure the effect of garlic on cholesterol. The cholesterol reduction proved succesful; however, patients in the study also reported "measurably less fatigue, anxiety, sensitivity, agitation and irritability" (Carper, 1993, 291). It is no wonder that in Germany, where this study was conducted, garlic has the largest sales volume of all over-the-counter drugs.

GARLIC AND ULCERS

The phytochemicals in garlic are also appreciated in Korea. At the Catholic University Medical College in Seoul, it was found that the diallyl disulfide and allicin in garlic caused the production of prostaglandins, which protect and strengthen the lining of the stomach, and may retard the development of ulcers (Carper, 1993).

THE LIST OF BENEFITS GOES ON

This is certainly not an exhaustive list of the many benefits of the phytochemicals found in garlic. They have been used to treat loose teeth, to remove tartar deposits, to treat polio, tuberculosis, ear infections, open wounds, typhus, asthma and whooping cough, and to remove toxic heavy metals like mercury, that prevent smooth functioning in the immune system (Crayhon, 1994).

Last, but certainly not least, Lloyd J. Harris found that garlic was used by the Roman aristocracy to remove sexual inhibitions and maximize sexual pleasure. The rabbis decreed that garlic should be eaten on the Sabbath, a night devoted to the marital "coming together." Sexually inhibited religions strictly forbade the eating of garlic, believing it created sexual desire.

Certainly there are many benefits to the phytochemicals found in garlic. The preceding research should encourage us to include garlic regularly in our diet, whether eaten in our foods or taken as a supplement, if we care about our health and well-being..

6 Cancer Prevention

"Just a few years ago, scientists didn't know phytochemicals existed. But today they are the new frontier in cancer-prevention research."
— Begley, 1994

Cancer is the second leading cause of death in the United States, deserving much of our attention regarding what we might do to prevent it. In 1993, there were 1,170,000 new cases of cancer reported. In 1994, it was estimated that there would be 1.2 million (Begley, 1994). Thirty-five percent of deaths related to cancer have been found to be diet-related (Doll and Peto, 1981).

There is substantial data now suggesting that our diet, in and of itself, can be a prevention to the dreaded disease of cancer. Gladys Block at the University of California at Berkeley's School of Public Health stated: "People whose diets are rich in fruits and vegetables are less likely to get cancers of the lung, stomach, colon, bladder, pancreas, esophagus, mouth, larynx, cervix, ovary, endometrium and breast" (*Health Horizons*, 1993).

CANCER REDUCTION THROUGH DIETARY CHANGES

The importance of our diet, specifically eating fruits and vegetables, cannot be overemphasized. *Life Extension Update* has reported that if we were to increase our intake of vegetables such as cabbage and broccoli on a daily basis, we would see a dramatic reduction in the cancer rate in the United States (Gordon, 1994). Tim Byers from the Centers for Disease Control and Prevention in Atlanta, Georgia, stated: "There's an explosion of compelling and consistent data associating diets rich in fruits and vegetables with a lower cancer risk" (Napier, 1995, p. 9).

THE DIET AND CANCER PROJECT

The AICR (American Institute for Cancer Research) and the WCFR (World Cancer Research Fund) joined forces with 15 renowned scientists to embark on a "Diet and Cancer Project." The goals of this project are to review literature which links food, nutrition and cancer risk; to make dietary recommendations to hopefully reduce cancer risk; to evaluate any links to cancer prevention and heart disease prevention; and to find creative ways to implement these recommendations. To date, there have been four meetings to discuss dietary recommendations. After a recent meeting in Mexico City, it was stated: "The dietary evidence continues to support AICR's current recommendations to eat a diet rich in vegetables, fruits and whole grains, and to drink alcohol in moderation, if at all. There appears to be practically no limit to the health benefits of such a diet" (*American Institute for Cancer Research* Newsletter, Fall 1995, 5).

DIET AND TUMOR PREVENTION

There have been at least 200 epidemiologic studies in the United States and literally all over the world which have found a radical link between a diet rich in fruits and vegetables and a lower incidence of tumors (Napier, 1995). The phytochemicals in fruits and vegetables obviously play a major role in this cancer prevention. Dr. Clare Hasler, at the only full-scale scientific program devoted to identifying and studying these phytochemicals, at the University of Illinois, noted, "Phytochemicals and other dietary substances no doubt work in concert to fight cancer and other diseases" (Napier, 1995, p. 12). Scientists and researchers all over the world are beginning to study the mysteries of the powers of these phytochemicals to prevent cancer.

ARE WE RESPONSIBLE WITH OUR DIET AND HEALTH CARE?

"A previously hidden world of natural chemicals in edible plants is unfolding, and the more researchers learn, the more certain they are that Mom was right: we should eat our vegetables, and lots of them" (Napier, 1995, p. 9). Yet getting us to do this is a major chore. Our resistance to taking care of our health has been noted in many studies conducted by numerous cancer institutes and research groups (Light et al., 1989).

One such study was targeted at providing education information at point-of-purchase (P-O-P). The study developed one minute video-taped PSAs (public service announcements) regarding diet and the reduction in the risk of cancer development. These video tapes were then played in the produce department at a supermarket at peak shopping times. Interviewers were stationed at store exits to interview shoppers as they were leaving the store. Only 26 percent of those interviewed had viewed the videotape. Of the 74 percent who didn't, various reasons were given. For example, 33 percent stated they didn't have time, 24 percent stated they didn't notice the tape, nine percent admitted to paying no attention to the tape, and seven percent just were not interested. Of those who did view the tapes, 43 percent acknowledged that the information was new to them.

However, only 21 percent of the meager 26 percent who had viewed the video tape agreed to change their eating habits (Cotugna and Vickery, 1992).

BREAST CANCER PREVENTION

Hopefully, you who are reading this chapter are among the 21 percent who will agree to change your eating habits. The evidence is in our favor. One study found that women who ate few fruits and vegetables were at 25 percent greater risk of developing breast cancer (Napier, 1995). In compiling the results of 23 studies, it was found that diets high in grain and vegetables reduced the risk of colon cancer a remarkable 40 percent (Napier, 1995).

As these and other studies note, there is a huge benefit in changing our diet and adding plenty of fruits and vegetables. Many of us would like to think that simply adding a daily vitamin to our morning coffee routine would do the trick. Yet the evidence is overwhelmingly stacked that we need to consume fruits and vegetables. "Vegetables like these contain a wide range of chemopreventive compounds that go way beyond vitamins" (Gordon, 1994, p. 32). However, there are companies that are flash-freeze-drying fruits and vegetables and encapsulating their phytochemicals. "Phytochemicals could be our vitamins of the future" (Schardt, 1994, 1).

Exactly which of these phytochemicals are cancer preventives and exactly how they work is still the subject of many studies. However, some information is beginning to emerge from the research to answer these questions.

We do know that the phytochemicals, or functional components of these phytochemicals, interact with each step in the multi-step process of cancer development. Some of the phytochemicals slow the development, some stop it, and some actually reverse it.

PHYTOCHEMICALS BLOCK CARCINOGENS

One specific thing we know that the phytochemicals do is boost the production and/or activity of enzymes that are blocking agents and suppressing agents to cancer cells. The blocking agents actually detoxify carcinogens or keep them from penetrating cells. (Carcinogens are those compounds that can give rise to cancer by disrupting the genetic pattern in our cells. These cells are programmed to be healthy, but when a carcinogen enters the genetic pattern, abnormal cells are created). The suppressing agents prevent malignant changes in cells that are exposed to carcinogens.

SULPHORAPHANE AS A CANCER PREVENTIVE

Sulphoraphane, found in broccoli, kale and radishes, is not only a potent activator of, but actually boosts the activity of "phase 2 enzymes." These "phase 2 enzymes" detoxify carcinogens, and hook them up to molecules that seem to have wheels. Therefore, broccoli ejects carcinogens before they can reek havoc on the healthy genetic code in our cells (Begley, 1994; Crabb, 1995). More simply, Dr. Paul Talalay of Johns Hopkins University School of Medicine, stated that "it works by causing cells to expel cancer-causing toxins" (*Times-Dispatch*, 1992).

This was actually discovered by feeding experimental mice sulphoraphane for five days. It was found that the increase of this phytochemical in their bodies triggered enzymes that are known to neutralize carcinogens in cells, rendering them unable to cause cancer.

CAROTENOIDS AS CANCER PREVENTIVES

Carotenoids, found in carrots, sweet potatoes, kale, cantaloupe, parsley, spinach and cauliflower, are excellent in their antioxidant action. They improve the communication among healthy cells, which is believed to prevent cancer cells from taking over. Beta carotene can also be converted into retinoic acid. The retinoic acid is believed to control genes that have a significant impact on whether or not cancer is developed. The increase in retinoic acid apparently sends out messages to the control genes to stop or to prevent the development of cancer (Napier, 1995).

FOLIC ACID AS A CANCER PREVENTIVE

Folate, or folic acid, found in turnip greens, okra,

spinach, kidney beans, asparagus, avocados, Brussels sprouts, lima beans, chickpeas, oranges, beets and raspberries, helps our body form healthy red blood cells. Studies have shown that people with higher levels of folic acid have less risk of developing colon cancer or polyps. Folate also supports the building of healthy tissue by standing guard over the healthy genetic messages encoded in our DNA. If carcinogens are allowed to invade our DNA, cancer develops and spreads (Napier, 1995).

ALLICIN AS A CANCER PREVENTIVE

Allicin, found in garlic and onions, has long been noted as a cancer preventive (*Better Nutrition for Today's Living*, May, 1995). Allicin is in a family of chemical compounds called phytoalexins. Their purpose in plants is to protect them from pathogenic invaders and insects. In humans, it stops aflatoxin (a carcinogen from food molds) from binding to our DNA. It also inhibits an enzyme called ADA (adenosine deaminase), which can bind carcinogens to our DNA. In addition, the organosulfur compounds found in garlic and onions block and suppress cancer-causing agents.

CALCIUM AS A CANCER PREVENTIVE

Calcium, found in collards, figs, turnip greens, kale, broccoli, okra and pinto beans, is a known preventive to colon cancer. It acts by inhibiting growth of unhealthy cells.

This renders potential toxins ineffective by binding them to fatty acids instead of allowing them to invade healthy cells, attempting to alter our healthy DNA cell programming.

FLAVONOIDS AS A CANCER PREVENTIVE

Flavonoids are cancer-fighting phytochemicals found in most plants. It is the flavonoids that give plants their rich color. They also have excellent antioxidant properties. They block the entrance of carcinogens into cells and also suppress cells from converting to malignant cell production. In addition, they interrupt the ability of hormones to bind to cells. When hormones do bind to cells, cancer can develop.

OTHER CANCER PREVENTING PHYTOCHEMICALS

Indoles, found in kale, Brussels sprouts, cabbage and broccoli, actually serve as scavengers in the body, seeking out cancer-causing substances. When they find carcinogens, they block them before they ever get to the cells they are seeking to attack.

Oltipraz, found in cabbage, causes an enzyme known as glutathione-S-transferase to increase. This enzyme works to protect liver cells against cancer. In experiments conducted using animals, it also has been shown to protect against colon, breast, stomach and skin cancer.

Whether or not we understand the exact chemical makeup of these compounds or understand exactly how they work, the bottom line is the same: if we care about our health and the health of those we love, we must take a serious look at our intake of fruits and vegetables. For many, taking a look would only be the first step, followed by an increase in our consumption of both fruits and vegetables.

7 Lung Cancer: The Preventative Effect of Fruits & Vegetables

"Eating one extra carrot a day might help prevent from 15,000 to 20,000 lung cancer deaths a year."
— Dr. Marilyn Menkes, Johns Hopkins University

It was predicted that in 1994, there would be 171,000 Americans who would contract lung cancer (Sherry, 1994). In the last 25 years, there has been a 185 percent increase in incidence among men and a 239 percent increase among women (Salaman and Scheer, 1994). Lung cancer now is the leading cause of cancer death among women (Walker and Brin, 1988).

The diagnosis of cancer is most frequent in those aged 55 to 60. However, in recent years, there has been a threefold increase in the diagnoses among those aged 40-45, and a ten-fold increase in those aged 60 to 65.

According the the American Cancer Society, cigarette smoking causes 75 percent of all lung cancers in women and 85 percent of all lung cancers in men. There are other causes of lung cancer, such as exposure to toxic herbicides and insecticides; chronic lung weakness from bronchitis or TB (Rector-Page, 1992); industrial exposure to chemicals such a uranium, nickle chromates, vinyl chloride and asbestos; outdoor pollution; and "passive smoking" (the exposure to cigarette smoke from others who are smoking).

Smoking and poor diet are among the top ten risk factors for developing disease in the United States, according to the United States Department of Health and Human Services, Office of Disease Prevention and Health Promotion (1986). Cigarette smokers are nine times more likely to contract lung cancer than are those who have never smoked. Those who smoke cigars are at 1.8 times greater risk, and those who smoke pipes are at 2.2 times greater risk. Those who are "passive smokers," particularly those who live with smokers, are at 1.5 times greater risk of developing lung cancer than those who do not smoke (Sherry, 1994). It is because of these risks that in 1964, the Surgeon General began requiring all packaging for cigarettes to carry a warning label.

SMOKERS EAT LESS FRUITS AND VEGETABLES

The high risk of lung cancer that is associated with smoking is further complicated and compounded by an interesting finding: smokers eat less fruits and vegetables, which are known to have cancer-preventive properties. In addition, it has been discovered that intake of fruits and vegetables goes down in smokers as their smoking increases (Subar et al., 1990). "Smokers, who are known to be at increased risk for several cancers, have lower intake of nutrients and foods associated with cancer prevention than non-smokers" (Subar et al, 1990, 1328).

The good news is that those smokers who do manage to keep their intake of fruits and vegetables up have less chance of developing lung cancer than those smokers who do not keep their intake up (Byers et al., 1987). Smoking tends to decrease the desire for sweet foods, including fruits and fruit juices (Grunberg, 1982). This could reduce or eliminate the desire for drinking orange juice, a significant fighter of lung cancer.

VITAMIN C PROTECTS THE LUNGS

The vitamin C in orange juice protects against cancer in three ways. First, it can prevent carcinogens from forming and amassing in the first place. Secondly, it can decrease the carcinogenic effects of some chemical agents. And finally, it has properties which can enhance our host resistance (Block and Menkes, 1988).

Another interesting biochemical note is that research has indicated that the vitamin C turnover is higher in smokers than in nonsmokers. Although smokers might take in the RDA (Recommended Daily Allowance) of vitamin C, it may be used up in their system more quickly. Not only do smokers need more vitamin C than do nonsmokers, but research indicates that they consume less (Subar et al., 1990).

STOP SMOKING!

The obvious solution is to STOP SMOKING. Being a psychotherapist and having practiced many years in the area of addictions, I am aware that stopping the cigarette habit is easier said than done. However, now, more than ever before, the market is flooded with resources to assist in the process — everything from acupuncture to nicorette gum to the "patch."

Even when smoking is stopped, the risk for lung cancer does not automatically disappear. The risk does decline steadily for fifteen years until the risk is similar to that of nonsmokers (Sherry, 1994). "SMOKING HAS BEEN CALLED THE NUMBER ONE REVERSIBLE CAUSE OF DEATH IN THE WORLD" (Cawood, 1995, 385). Smoking may be pleasurable for the moment, but the long-term consequences are horrific. "Smokers live shorter lives and die more painful and prolonged deaths" (Salaman and Scheer, 1994, 148). If you absolutely refuse to stop smoking, make it a resolution to increase your intake of fruits and vegetables.

FRUIT AND VEGETABLE CONSUMPTION LOWERS RISK OF LUNG CANCER

There is clear evidence linking fruit consumption to a lower risk of lung cancer (Fraser et al., 1991). Of 32 studies on diet and lung cancer conducted in recent years, 30 of those studies indicated fruits and vegetables to be powerful food antidotes (Carper, 1993).

One such study was conducted in California, using Seventh-day Adventists as subjects. They were selected because they have been shown to have a lower mortality rate from lung cancer than similar non-Adventists in the general population (Phillips et al., 1978). There are also many Seventh-day Adventists who are vegetarians. Part of their religious regimen is that they are not supposed to smoke or drink, and they are encouraged to exercise (*Consumer Reports on Health*, October, 1995). For the study, 34,198 Seventh-day Adventists were chosen, of which only 4 percent were smokers. After six years, only 61 cases of lung cancer were reported. "Fruit consumption was the dietary constituent that showed a strong, statistically significant protective association with lung cancer that was independent of smoking" (Fraser et al., 1991, 683).

BETA CAROTENE AND LUNG CANCER

In another study involving Chicago men, 1,954 of the men were followed for 19 years. Those who ate foods rich in beta carotene, such as carrots, dark green lettuce, spinach, broccoli, kale, cabbage, peaches and apricots, had lower rates of lung cancer than men in similar control groups (Shekelle et al., 1981).

In a New Jersey study, nonsmokers who lived and/or worked around smokers (making them "passive smokers") cut their risk of contracting lung cancer by one-half by simply adding an extra half cup of dark-yellow and orange vegetables to their diets on a daily basis.

Another study in Hong Kong showed that passive smokers who ate carrots reduced their risk of lung cancer by 90 percent. Those who ate fresh green leafy vegetables cut their risk by 70 percent and those who ate fresh fruit cut theirs by 40 percent (Carper, 1993).

Dr. Marilyn Menkes of Johns Hopkins University conducted a follow-up study of persons whose blood had been tested for beta carotene levels in 1974. Nine years later, she followed up on these individuals, and found that those whose blood tested to be low in beta carotene in 1974 had two times the lung cancer rate. Not only that, but their beta carotene levels proved to be a predictor of squamous cell carcinoma, a sort of skin cancer in the lining of the lungs, known to be the most deadly lung cancer among smokers. Those with the lowest levels of beta carotene in the 1974 study had a four-times greater chance of contracting squamous cell carcinoma than those who had higher levels of beta carotene in the 1974 study (Carper, 1993).

FRUITS AND VEGETABLES IN THE TREATMENT OF LUNG CANCER

Not only are fruits and vegetables preventives in regard to lung cancer, they also have shown some treatment benefits. "New research shows that food substances, such as beta carotene, can attack and destroy tumor cells and retard the growth and spread of tumors" (Carper, 1993, p. 254).

In one study, 463 males and 212 females, all lung cancer patients, were followed. The women who ate lots of vegetables, especially broccoli, doubled their survival time. They survived about 33 months, as compared to the 18-month survival time of those who ate the least fruits and vegetables. Men who increased their consumption of oranges and tomatoes also increased their survival time (Carper, 1993).

Not to preempt any medical treatment, but certainly as an addition to it, fruit and vegetable consumption should be increased by any and all cancer patients. "A recent report from the University of Hawaii's Cancer Research Center in Honolulu indicated that vegetables' chemotherapeutic powers stifled cancer progression and virulence and prolonged survival time" (Carper, 1993, 254).

Beta carotene acts as a powerful antioxidant and also enhances immunological defenses that can fight and prevent cancer. However, beta carotene is not the only phytochemical effective in the fight against and prevention of lung cancer. Folate, or folic acid, can strengthen and protect chromosomes from breaking. (When they break they are more susceptible to carcinogenic invasion). Lutein, lycopene, and indole have all been shown to act with beta carotene in effective lung cancer prevention. Beta carotene was shown to reduce risk of lung cancer three times among women and two times among men. When all phytochemicals were ingested, women experienced seven times less risk of developing lung cancer, and men were three times less likely to develop lung cancer (Carper, 1993).

IT DOESN'T TAKE MUCH

It doesn't take large amounts of fruits and vegetables to give us these positive benefits. A single raw carrot twice a week reduces the risk of lung cancer 60 percent. A cup of raw broccoli twice weekly reduces the risk 70 percent. A cup of raw spinach twice weekly reduces the risk by 40 percent (Carper, 1993). "Amazingly, research suggests that eating only an extra single carrot, a half cup of dark yellow-orange or dark green vegetables, a piece of fruit or a glass of juice daily, or even more than once a week, could mean the difference between getting and not getting lung cancer" (Carper, 1993, 247). The evidence is before us; the decision is ours.

8 Colon Cancer: The Effects of Fruits & Vegetables

"If you choose your menu wisely, you can actually build a line of defense against cancer."
— *Book of Proven Home Remedies and Natural Healing Secrets*

Colon cancer is second only to lung cancer as a major cause of death among males in America (*Better Nutrition for Today's Living*, "Health Watch," May, 1995). It is estimated that six percent of the American population will eventually develop colon cancer. It appears to occur equally in males and females, and the incidence increases gradually as people reach age 40 (Sherry, 1994).

It was predicted that 152,000 cases of colon cancer would be diagnosed in the United States in 1994 (Sherry, 1994). In the United States, an average of 100,000 people die annually due to colon cancer. Overweight men seem to be particularly at risk (Rector-Page, 1992). The incidence of colon cancer is higher among women who have previously had breast, ovarian or endometrial cancers. People with ulcerative colitis are also at greater risk (Fitzsimmons and Fales, 1993).

A HOPEFUL NOTE ABOUT COLON CANCER PREVENTION

Although the statistics above are frightening, there is a hopeful note. It has been noted that 90 percent of colon cancer could be influenced and/or prevented by dietary factors (Carper, 1993). The etiologic factors are strongly related to nutrition, specifically to the intake of fiber, fat and vegetables, and how they are cooked (Weisburger, 1991). Diets low in fiber intake and high in fat consumption promote colon cancer, whereas diets high in fiber (such as vegetables and antioxidants) inhibit cancer, whether or not the fat intake is altered (Fitzsimmons and Fales, 1993).

The fibers found most effective in colon cancer prevention are insoluble fibers, such as found in carrots, celery and wheat bran cereals. These fibers bind with water, which increases fecal bulk, moving it on through the system in a shorter time. This is critical to colon cancer prevention, because the longer fecal waste is stored in the large intestine, the greater the chance of cancer-causing substances beginning to form (Salaman and Scheer, 1994).

FRUITS AND VEGETABLES PROTECT AGAINST COLON CANCER

In a project reviewing 21 studies regarding diet and colon cancer, there were some definitive conclusions drawn. Thirteen of the studies strongly supported the notion that fruits, vegetables and fiber provide a protective effect against colon cancer. The other eight studies provided moderate support for their protective effect. "Critical evaluation of epidemiologic studies of fiber and colon cancer provides considerable evidence that a diet rich in fiber and vegetables is associated with a reduced risk of colon cancer" (Trock et al., 1990, 658).

BETA CAROTENE AND COLON CANCER

Beta carotene and wheat bran fiber are two of the most often cited preventives for colon cancer. In one thirty-week study, rats were fed a high fat diet with low amounts of wheat bran and beta carotene in what they were fed. A second group was fed a high fat diet with large amounts of wheat bran fiber and beta carotene in their diet. Another group was given a high fat diet only and was watched and monitored for comparison. Following this stage, they were all given carcinogens believed to cause colon cancer. The results demonstrated that when wheat bran fiber and beta carotene are increased in the diet, the incidence of precancerous colon cells, polyps and tumors decreased. This held true even in those rats given high fat diets (Alabaster et al., 1995).

DIETARY PREDICTORS OF COLON CANCER

At the Harvard School of Public Health, a group of men were studied to determine the dietary predictors of colon cancer. It was observed that men with the lowest fat intake had about 50 percent less risk of colon cancer than those who ate average amounts of fat in their diet. For prevention, it was recommended that six servings of whole grains and legumes and five to six servings of fruits and vegetables be eaten on a daily basis (*Boston Globe*, 1991).

In a Norwegian study, 155 people in their 50s who had no diagnosis or symptoms of colon cancer were examined medically. About half of them had colon polyps, an early indicator of possible colon cancer. The other half had none. Those without the polyps reportedly consumed more cruciferous vegetables than those who had polyps (Jack, 1991).

In another study, 88,751 female nurses were studied over a ten year period of time. Those who were free of colon cancer, once again, were those who consumed a diet high in fiber, fruits and vegetables. This investigation found apples and pears to be the fiber fruits providing the most protection (Willett, 1990).

At the Graham State University of New York at Buffalo, 256 male colon cancer patients were investigated. When compared to controls, it was obvious that the colon cancer patients had little or no regular intake of vegetables. Those controls who had consumed the most vegetables had the least risk of colon cancer (Salaman and Scheer, 1994).

CABBAGE AND OTHER CRUCIFEROUS VEGETABLES AS COLON CANCER PREVENTIVES

In New York, another study focused on a male population. The men who ate cabbage more than one time weekly were 66 percent less likely to develop colon cancer when compared to those who ate cabbage only once a month. Eating cabbage only every two to three weeks cut the risk of colon cancer in half. The researchers speculated that it was the indoles in cabbage, also present in other cruciferous vegetables, that provided the protective effect (Carper, 1993).

In a similar type of study, 600 men at the University of Utah School of Medicine were evaluated according to their diet. Men who ate the most cruciferous vegetables had a 70 percent lower risk of developing colon cancer (Carper, 1993).

GARLIC AND COLON CANCER

Garlic, once again ranking high in its phytochemical benefits, has been found effective in preventing colon cancer tumors. In an experiment involving laboratory animals, it was noted that approximately 80 percent of colon cancer tumors were prevented with intake of garlic (*Medical Tribune*, 1994).

PECTIN AS A PREVENTIVE OF COLON CANCER

At the University of Texas Health Science Center in San Antonio, rats were used to examine the preventive effects of diet in relation to colon cancer. When their diets were supplemented with pectin (found in apples, pears, prunes, apricots, carrots, dried beans and the white membrane of citrus fruits), the rates of colon cancer dropped 50 percent (Carper, 1993).

Reviewing many of these studies, a doctor at the University of Toronto predicted that if Americans ate an additional 13 grams of cereal, fruits, vegetables and legumes daily, our colon cancer rate would drop 31 percent (Carper, 1993). It is our choice. We can take the evidence to heart and be among the 31 percent, or we can choose to ignore the facts. Choose fruits, vegetables and grains.

9 Breast Cancer: Diet-Related Prevention & Treatment

"To escape breast cancer, eat more like Asian women."
— Jean Carper

Breast cancer is the cancer which receives more attention in the popular press than any of the other cancers. Popular magazines, radio talk shows and television talk shows are filled with articles and news regarding breast cancer. According to the American Cancer Society, 182,000 cases of breast cancer are diagnosed annually in the United States. Forty percent of those diagnosed die. Sixty-six percent of breast cancer occurs in post-menopausal women. It strikes most women between the ages of 40 and 50, and is the leading cause of death among women (Sherry, 1994).

There are a number of risk factors for breast cancer with which women should be familiar. They include factors such as: never having given birth, giving birth to the first child after the age of 30, early sexual maturing, having a mother or sister with breast cancer, having a history of cysts in breasts, being overweight, and being over age 40 (Cawood, 1993).

DEFENDING YOURSELF AGAINST BREAST CANCER

There are ways to defend yourself against breast cancer. The primary defenses are to cut the intake of fat, to add fruits and vegetables to your diet (cutting the risk 50 percent), to lose weight, to breast-feed your children (breast feeding your first or second child one to six months cuts the risk 10 to 25 percent) and to do regular self-examinations (Harder, 1986).

LOWERING THE INTAKE OF FAT TO REDUCE THE RISK OF BREAST CANCER

All of these lines of defense are quite significant. However, cutting the intake of fat has been one of the most difficult things for busy women in our culture to do. It has been predicted that if American women cut their daily saturated fat intake to one-tenth of their total caloric intake, the rate of breast cancer occurrence for post-menopausal women would drop at least ten percent (Cawood, 1993).

In a review of studies, compiled information demonstrated the critical importance of lowering fat intake. When intake of fat was lowered in the diets of women over the period of a month, the risk of contracting breast cancer was lowered, the severity of the disease was lessened and there was an increase in the cure rate following surgery in those with breast cancer (Cawood, 1993).

In a study involving 2,300 Israeli women, the importance of a low fat diet was again emphasized. The study found that those with a diet high in fat were three times more likely to develop tumors that led to breast cancer (Cawood, 1993).

FRUITS AND VEGETABLES AS A LINE OF DEFENSE AGAINST BREAST CANCER

Defending ourselves by increasing our intake of fruits and vegetables is a matter of critical importance, in addition to lowering our fat intake. "To boost your protection against breast cancer, eat fruits and vegetables, especially those high in vitamin C, instead of fat" (Cawood, 1993, 97). Vitamin C does seem to be one of the critical preventives for breast cancer. "Just by eating enough fruits and vegetables to get 380 milligrams of vitamin C daily might drop the breast cancer rate by another 16 percent for all women over age 20" (Cawood, 1993, 97). In a review of 12 studies, the data noted that vitamin C was the number one protector against breast cancer. As a matter of fact, the studies noted that too little vitamin C was more critical than a diet high in fat (Carper, 1993). "Vitamin C is a formidable antagonist to breast cancer" (Carper, 1993, 228).

CRUCIFEROUS VEGETABLES AND BREAST CANCER

Cruciferous vegetables, once again, play an important role in breast cancer. Asian women, who typically eat more cruciferous vegetables than American women, have a much lower rate of breast cancer than women in the United States. Cruciferous vegetables contain indole-3-carbinol. This phytochemical appears to be able to convert the estrogen which promotes cancer into a benign estrogen. When the equivalent of 500 milligrams of cruciferous vegetables was eaten daily, the production of the chemical that blocks dangerous estrogen increased 50 percent (Cawood, 1993). Cabbage, broccoli, cauliflower, Brussels sprouts, mustard greens, turnips and kale, all cruciferous vegetables containing indoles, speed up the metabolism of estrogen, moving it out quickly, before it has an opportunity to feed cancer. "Specific indoles in these cruciferous vegetables accelerate a process in which the body deactivates or disposes of the type of estrogen that can promote breast cancer" (Carper, 1993, 222).

Breast, uterine and ovarian cancers are all hormone-dependent. Tamoxifen is a prescription drug given to women with hormone-dependent cancers to lessen the effects of estrogen. Eating cruciferous vegetables can manipulate estrogen in the same way.

BEANS AND BREAST CANCER

Beans, particularly pinto beans, garbanzo beans and black beans, contain phytoestrogens that stop the activity of cancer-causing estrogens. Hispanic women have less breast cancer, and they eat beans an average of six days a week. Typical Caucasian women eat beans less than half that often, averaging two days weekly (Carper, 1993).

GREEN VEGETABLES AND BREAST CANCER

All green vegetables are important when addressing our line of defense against breast cancer. In a study of Italian women, it was noted that those who ate more than one green vegetable a day had only one-third the risk of developing breast cancer than the women who ate less than that amount (Carper, 1993).

GARLIC AND BREAST CANCER

The phytochemicals in garlic, such as diallyl disulfide and S-allylcysteine, have proven to be very effective in preventing and treating breast cancer. Although some of the initial work on using these phytochemicals found in garlic to prevent and treat breast cancer used dogs as experimental animals, it was later found that the phytochemicals were even more effective in treating breast cancer in humans (Murray, 1994).

SELENIUM AND BREAST CANCER

Selenium is another phytochemical that has gained attention in the cancer-preventive studies. Selenium is found in foods such as corn, cabbage, whole wheat, beans, peas, onions, beets, tomatoes, garlic, brown rice and peanuts. One predictor of breast cancer is low levels of selenium. At the University of California at San Diego, rats were studied to note the effect of selenium on breast cancer. Trace amounts of selenium were added daily to the drinking water of rats which were at high risk of developing breast cancer. Another group of rats which were at high risk was given regular drinking water. The rate of breast cancer incidence among those given selenium dropped from 82 percent to 10 percent (Kunin, 1981).

The same study also gathered blood from blood banks in 17 nations to measure selenium levels. The levels in Asian and Latin American countries were three times higher than those in North American and European countries. It is not surprising to note the death rates from breast cancer are two to five times higher in the North American and European countries than in Asian and Latin American countries (Kunin, 1981). It is critical that we bolster our defenses by eating those foods high in selenium or by taking supplemental selenium.

FRUITS AND VEGETABLES PREVENT SPREADING OF BREAST CANCER

Fruit and vegetable consumption is not only important in the prevention of breast cancer, it is also important in preventing the spreading of cancer once it has been diagnosed. This is very significant because metastasis (the spread of tumors to a secondary site) is actually the cause of death in most cancer patients. In a laboratory study, animals were injected with breast cancer cells. One group of animals ate diets high in cabbage and collard greens. A month later, that group had only half as many lung tumors as those fed a diet without cabbage and collard greens (Cawood, 1993).

The problem is that many women don't seem to care for the taste of cabbage, collard greens, turnips and other such flavorful vegetables. "The problem is one of taste - many people just don't like to eat their veggies, especially broccoli and Brussels sprouts. Dr. Jon J. Michnovicz, one of the researchers who found the cancer fighter, suggests that indole-3-carbinol could be sold in a pill form" (Cawood, 1993, 103). There are now such "pills" available. (See appendix for information about these pills and where they can be obtained).

The bottom line is that we, as women, need to pay attention to and act on the defenses that are available to us. Carper (1993) has summarized it well for us: "Eat a variety of green vegetables, which generally seems to deter breast cancer" (232).

10 Prostate, Stomach, Pancreatic & Skin Cancers: Can Fruits & Vegetables Help?

Fortunately, no one needs to wait for the results of further research to benefit from the many healthful ingredients in produce. They're available now in their natural packing at any grocery store.
— *Consumer Reports on Health*, February 1995

PROSTATE CANCER

Prostate cancer is the second most common cancer among American men. It has been called a disease of the elderly because the average age of diagnosis is 73. Only two percent of those diagnosed with the disease are under age 50. It was predicted that 165,000 cases of prostate cancer would be diagnosed in 1994 (Sherry, 1994). When diagnosed early, the disease is highly treatable.

There are mixed results regarding studies addressing the efficacy of fruits and vegetables with prostate cancer. More recent studies have shown that an increase in the intake of beta carotene decreases the risk of prostate cancer, with the exception of men over the age of seventy. One study indicated that there was a positive association between prostate cancer and the intake of papaya (LeMarchand et al., 1991).

An earlier study conducted by some of the same research team had indicated a positive association between beta carotene and prostate cancer (Kolonel et al., 1987). When repeating the study, the specific fruits containing beta carotene were investigated independently, and it was found that some phytochemical in papaya, not beta carotene, was the culprit (LeMarchand et al., 1991). "Since beta carotene is not unique to papaya, our results suggests that beta carotene alone is unlikely to be responsible for the positive correlation" (LeMarchand et al., 1991, 217).

The lycopene in tomatoes appears to be effective in defending the body against prostate cancer. In a study conducted in California with Seventh-day Adventist men, it was found that tomato consumption had a protective effect against the development of prostate cancer (Mills et al., 1989).

Zinc also appears to be helpful in defending the body against prostate cancer. At the Cook County Hospital in Chicago, 755 prostate cancer patients were examined and blood levels were drawn. It was found that those patients had lower zinc levels than the normal population (Faelten, 1981). Zinc is in food such as beets, seafoods, soybeans, whole grain wheat bread and walnuts.

Vitamin D, which we primarily get from exposure to sunshine, appears to slow the growth of prostate cancer cells. When human prostate tumors were grafted onto mice and they were given vitamin D, the growth rate of the tumors slowed down considerably (Feldman, 1994). This vitamin was found to be a prostate cancer preventative at Stanford University in Palo Alto, California, as well.

Studies from Duke University have reported similar results when investigating prostate cancer and vitamin D. They studied 181 men who had been diagnosed with prostate cancer, and found that they had lower levels of vitamin D than men who had no cancer diagnosis (*Better Nutrition for Today's Living*, March, 1995).

STOMACH CANCER

Stomach cancer tends to occur most often in older people, probably because one of the major causes is the lack of fiber intake. Stomach cancer takes a long time to develop, sometimes as long as 15 years. Other causes of stomach cancer include: a diet high in fat, high intake of red meat, HCL (hydrochloride) deficiency and "low intake of fresh fruits, vegetables and olive oil" (Rector-Page, 1992, p. 167).

The rates of stomach cancer are especially high in

Japan. Most scientists and dieticians have believed the rate was high as a result of the large intake of soy sauce. However, in a study conducted with mice at the University of Wisconsin, the test animals were given a diet high in fermented soy sauce. Not only did they have a 26 percent lower cancer rate than mice on regular diets, but they also had one-fourth the number of tumors as the control group (Raloff, 1991). The soy sauce seemed to have anticarcinogenic properties.

The Chinese also have a high rate of stomach cancer. However, according to the National Institute of Cancer, those Chinese who eat significant amounts of garlic and onion tend to have about one-fourth the rate of stomach cancer of other Chinese (Cawood, 1994). In one of these areas known for high stomach cancer rates in China, a study compared 564 patients with stomach cancer to 1,131 control patients. Those who increased their intake of allium (through garlic and onions) had significantly fewer stomach cancer occurrences (You et al., 1989).

In one area of Georgia, known for their production of Vidalia onions, the stomach cancer mortality rate is about one-third of that of the rest of the nation (Byers et al., 1990). This is further indication that the phytochemicals in onions can have a cancer-preventive effect.

Once again, the value of the intake of fruits and vegetables with this cancer is evident. For the health of our digestive system, an increase in our intake of fruits and vegetables is an absolute must!

PANCREATIC CANCER

Pancreatic cancer occurs less in heavy fruit eaters than it does in the general population (Carper, 1993). Diet is especially important in pancreatic cancer. "Eating to prevent pancreatic cancer can be critical because this cancer is especially resistant to treatment" (Carper, 1993, 256).

The highest rate of pancreatic cancer in the United States is among the Cajun population in Louisiana. A study noted that those who ate the most pork in their diets had the highest rates of pancreatic cancer. Those who ate pork daily had a 70 percent greater chance of developing pancreatic cancer than those who ate it only twice a week. Those who ate pork more than once daily increased their risk for developing pancreatic cancer three times. Those who ate fruit twice daily were only 40 percent as likely to develop this cancer. The more fruit they consumed, the lower the risk of pancreatic cancer. Not only did the fruit intake lower the risk, but it also seemed to counteract the risk the pork presented. Those who ate a lot of fruit with pork were no more likely to be diagnosed with pancreatic cancer than those people who increased their consumption of fruit while reducing their intake of pork (Carper, 1993).

In a Swedish study, the importance of eating citrus fruit to prevent pancreatic cancer was highlighted. It was surmised that eating one citrus fruit daily could cut the risk of pancreatic cancer as much a one-half to two-thirds. In a similar study with Seventh-day Adventists, even dried fruit was shown to have a protective effect against pancreatic cancer (Carper, 1993).

In another study investigating the effect of specific fiber intake, the preventive effect of eating dried beans was studied. It was found that those who ate legumes weekly had a 40 percent less risk of developing pancreatic cancer. The result was believed to be due to the protease inhibitors found in the legumes (Carper, 1993).

One of the predictors of pancreatic cancer is low levels of lycopene. In a study at Johns Hopkins University, 26,000 people gave blood for various studies. Ten years later, the participants were followed up on, and it was found that those who had low levels of lycopene ten years earlier had a five times greater risk of pancreatic cancer (Carper, 1993). Lycopene is found in great quantity in tomatoes and watermelon.

"Bottom line: An orange or grapefruit a day may cut your chances of developing pancreatic cancer in half! People who don't eat tomatoes or watermelon are five times more likely to have pancreatic cancer" (Carper, 1993, 258).

SKIN CANCER

Skin cancer is the most common of all cancers. In 1993, there were 700,000 cases predicted in the United

States (Sherry, 1994). Skin cancer is rarely fatal and responds well to treatment if diagnosed early (Salaman and Scheer, 1994).

Basal cell skin cancer comprises 65 percent of skin cancer cases. These cases are normally males, over age 40, and the cure rate is 95 percent. Squamous cell cancer is the second most common skin cancer. It has a rapid growth rate, but the cure rate is 90 percent.

Melanoma tends to occur in younger patients, with men and women being at equal risk. By the year 2000, it is predicted that one in 75 Americans will develop melanoma. If diagnosed early, the cure rate is 95 percent. With late diagnosis, the cure rate drops to 30 percent (Sherry, 1994).

The risk factors for skin cancer are numerous and varied. They include such factors as: fair skin; freckles; blond, red or light brown hair; blue, green, grey eyes; tendency to sunburn; skin cancer in the family history; warm or sunny climate; intense exposure to sun and lots of moles (Cawood, 1994).

Once again, with this cancer, the intake of fruits and vegetables is quite significant. The antioxidants in fruits and vegetables seem to combat the ability of the omega-6 fats to promote the development of melanoma (Carper, 1993).

There is no doubt that the sun plays a major role in the development of skin cancer. However, fruits and vegetables can provide some combative effect. The ultraviolet rays of the sun cause the "in-skin" cholesterol to oxidize, which produces alpha-oxide, a cancer-causer. The vitamins C and E in fruits and vegetables guard against that oxidation process, in essence preventing the development of skin cancer. Increasing the intake of fruits and vegetables would reduce skin cancer cases to 50 percent of the current rate (Salaman and Scheer, 1994).

11 Heart Problems: Cardiovascular Disease, Blood Pressure & Cholesterol

*"A spiritual base in faith,
a daily exercise program,
a positive outlook and a diet of
much raw fruits and vegetables . . .
help keep my heart strong
and efficient and my health excellent."*
— Maureen Salaman

Our heart is such a critically important muscle within the walls of our chest. It pumps 600 thousand gallons of blood annually through 60 thousand miles of veins (Mandino, 1975). Not only does it pump our blood with life-sustaining oxygen through our bodies, but it is the place in our bodies we refer to when we speak of the feelings of love.

Heart disease comes in two varieties: 1) disorders

which are cardiovascular in nature, and 2) those which we refer to as "broken hearts." In the course of my practice, I spend much time doing healing work with the broken hearted; however, this chapter is addressing those disorders which are cardiovascular in nature.

Since as early as the 1960s, the American Heart Association has been attributing the major cause of cardiovascular disease to a faulty diet. "Most people in the United States consume more protein than they need. To lessen the risk of cardiovascular disease, the balance should be shifted in favor of a more complex carbohydrate, such as one found with fresh fruits and vegetables" (*The American Heart Association Heart Book*, 1980, 65).

VEGETARIANS AND HEART DISEASE

One of the most famous heart study projects conducted in our country is called the Framingham Heart Study. It is hailed as a great study due to the time frame and large numbers of participants it included. One aspect of the study investigated the heart conditions of 18,000 vegetarians living in California and compared them to others on a "normal diet" in the population at large. It was found that the vegetarians had an 85 percent lower occurrence of heart attacks, as well as a 60 percent lower rate of cancer. Men on the vegetarian diet lived an average of six to seven years longer, and women's average life spans were three years longer than the nonvegetarians (Jack, 1991).

HIGH BLOOD PRESSURE AND CHOLESTEROL PROBLEMS

It is very difficult to address cardiovascular disease without also incorporating blood pressure and cholesterol. High cholesterol (LDL levels) damages the walls of the arteries and plaque begins to build up, choking off the blood flow and elevating blood pressure. This combination of occurrences can lead to heart attacks and strokes. One thing that interrupts this whole process, according to research, is the presence of beta carotene in the diet.

At the Harvard Medical School, some male physicians who had been diagnosed with heart disease were asked to take beta carotene every other day for six years. Indeed, the artery-clogging process was slowed down. Those male doctors in the study, taking the supplemental beta carotene, had half as many heart attacks and strokes as those not supplementing with beta carotene (Cawood, 1993). Those in the group taking beta carotene experienced only 10 heart attacks; the other group reported 17 (*Boston Globe*, 1990).

ANGINA

Beta carotene levels are also significant in angina, heart pain that is often reported as a "chest-crushing" feeling. At the University of Edinburgh, 500 middle-aged men were studied. Half of them reported angina. After monitoring their blood levels, it was noted that those who had high levels of beta carotene, vitamin C and vitamin E were least likely to report chest pain. The prescription is simple and straightforward: "to alleviate angina, eat more fruits, vegetables, oily fish, cereals, nuts and vegetable oils rich in vitamin E" (Carper, 1993, 40).

GARLIC AND HEART DISEASE

As mentioned in earlier chapters, garlic is the miracle medicine saluted by many in preventing and in recovering from heart disease. This is understandable when reviewing the statistics resulting from studies with garlic eaters. Those who consume garlic regularly have a 32 percent lower incidence of heart attacks, and a 45 percent lower death rate when heart attacks do occur (Cawood, 1993).

Another key to preventing heart disease is to prevent the clotting which blocks the flow of blood. Clotting can particularly be a problem when any invasive surgery is performed. In one study, patients were given vitamin E and calcium prior to surgery. Another group was given only typical preparations for surgery. The group who received no vitamin E or calcium had two times more blood clots, six times more clots in the lungs and nine times more deaths resulting from blockages (Quillin, 1987). Garlic clearly plays a critical role in the prevention of clotting. Both garlic and onion seem to keep platelets slippery to abate their amassing into clots.

HYPERTENSION: HIGH BLOOD PRESSURE

An estimated 45 million Americans have mild to severe high blood pressure (Cawood, 1993). High blood pressure affects 10 to 20 percent of the adult population in the United States and is the leading cause of heart attacks, strokes and other cardiovascular diseases (Page, 1976).

High blood pressure that remains untreated can cause damage to the heart, arteries, kidneys, brain and eyes. People with uncontrolled blood pressure have seven times more strokes, four times more heart failures and three times more coronary heart disease than those people with normal blood pressure (Cawood, 1993).

CONTROLLING BLOOD PRESSURE WITH FRUITS AND VEGETABLES

There are numerous ways to control blood pressure. One is medication. However, there are some natural or alternative means of controlling blood pressure which can be done in conjunction with medication, or, with medical guidance, instead of medication. (That is a decision that must be made in cooperation with your medical doctor). The natural means include such choices as: losing weight if you are overweight, embarking on a mild exercise program, and altering or modifying your diet. It's a "Medical fact: there's something magic about a fruit- and vegetable-rich diet that curbs high blood pressure" (Carper, 1993, 87).

Daily fiber is a major contributor to lowering blood pressure. Fiber is found in wheat bran, oat bran, and in fruits and vegetables. However, the fiber in fruits and vegetables has more of an anti-hypertensive effect than the fiber in cereals. In a study done at Harvard, there were 31,000 middle-aged and elderly men observed. It was discovered that those who ate little fruit were 46 percent more likely to develop high blood pressure when compared to those who ate the fiber equivalent of five apples daily (Carper, 1993).

VITAMIN C AND HIGH BLOOD PRESSURE

The vitamin C component of various fruits and vegetables has been shown to be significant in lowering high blood pressure. Dr. Bulpitt, of the Hammersmith Hospital in London, is considered an expert in the field of hypertension. He found that high blood pressure and stroke fatalities were highest among those patients who ate the least amount of vitamin C (Carper, 1993). Those foods rich in vitamin C include: guava, red peppers, cantaloupe, papaya, strawberries, Brussels sprouts, grapefruit, kiwi fruit, oranges, broccoli, tomatoes, cauliflower and green peas.

CALCIUM AND HIGH SODIUM LEVELS: NO MORE SALT?

High salt intake, resulting in high sodium levels, has long been noted as a problem among those with high blood pressure. Surprisingly, foods high in calcium have been noted for reversing the effects of high sodium intake on blood pressure. Calcium prevents the release of the parathyroid hormone that can elevate blood pressure when sodium intake is high. For each 1,000 mg. of calcium taken in, blood pressure is lowered 20 to 40 percent in people who don't consume alcohol (Carper, 1993). (Alcohol counteracts calcium's ability to lower blood pressure). Calcium is found in foods such as: collards, dried figs, turnip greens, kale, broccoli, almonds, sesame seeds, okra and pinto beans. If you absolutely can't give up the salt, increase your intake of calcium. (The body absorbs calcium from calcium-fortified orange juice better than it does from milk).

POTASSIUM AND HIGH BLOOD PRESSURE

Other studies have accented the importance of potassium intake in relation to blood pressure. Low potassium has been linked to elevated blood pressure levels, and to a higher incidence of strokes (Cawood, 1993). One specific study indicated that high levels of potassium lowered the risk of stroke, no matter what the blood pressure levels were (Barrett-Carmen & Khan, 1984).

At a university in Italy, patients were put on a high potassium diet. After a year, 81 percent of the patients needed only half of the previous amount of prescribed medication to control their blood pressure. Thirty eight percent were able to stop all prescription medication for blood pressure (Carper, 1993).

Potassium-rich foods include such fruits and vegetables as: bananas, broccoli, avocados, Brussels sprouts, cauliflower, cantaloupe, prunes, spinach, apricots, tomato juice, orange juice and raisins. "The moral of the story — eat more fruits and vegetables to get more potassium" (Cawood, 1993, 82).

CELERY AND HIGH BLOOD PRESSURE

Another anti-hypertensive is a phytochemical found in celery. The 3-n-butyl phthalide was investigated at the University of Chicago's Pritzker School of Medicine. The phytochemical was extracted from the celery and was given to rats with normal blood pressure. Within a couple of weeks' time, their blood pressure, although already within normal range, was reduced 12 to 14 percent. In addition, their cholesterol levels dropped 14 percent.

Further research has proposed that the phytochemical in celery is effective because it reduces the levels of stress hormones in the blood, which causes vessel constriction. Therefore, celery and its phytochemicals may be most effective when blood pressure is elevated due to mental and emotional stress (Carper, 1993).

GARLIC AND HIGH BLOOD PRESSURE

Garlic once again comes to the forefront when investigating its phytochemical effects on blood pressure. In a German study, Kwai, a freeze-dried preparation of the valuable phytochemicals in garlic, was administered to patients with high blood pressure. The beginning blood pressure average was 171/102. After three months on Kwai, the average blood pressure was 152/89. The group that received a placebo treatment showed no change in blood pressure (Carper, 1993). There are five other significant studies that also indicate that garlic is effective in reducing blood pressure levels (Auer et al., 1990; Barrie et al., 1987; Grunwald, 1990; Kleijnen et al., 1989; McMahon and Vargas, 1993; Mansell and Reckless, 1991).

CAYENNE PEPPER AND HIGH BLOOD PRESSURE

Cayenne pepper also has been shown to reduce blood pressure and cholesterol levels (Sriniviesan et al., 1980). The phytochemical in cayenne pepper, capsaicin, seems to act in a reflexive manner, which assists in reducing blood pressure (Toh et al., 1955).

A MACROBIOTIC DIET AND HIGH BLOOD PRESSURE

The overall effect of eating fruits and vegetables was highlighted in a study at the Harvard Medical School. Macrobiotic eaters were evaluated and it was found that the females had an average blood pressure of 100.9/58.2. The males had an average of 109.7/60.9. Those who ate some seafood with their diet had higher blood pressures than those who ate a pure macrobiotic diet (Sacks et al., 1974).

CHOLESTEROL LEVELS

It seems that more commonly and more frequently, cholesterol levels are of major concern to many Americans. However, according to the Centers for Disease Control in Atlanta, Georgia, only 47 percent of Americans had had their blood pressure checked in the last year, and only six percent knew what their cholesterol levels were. Even of those who did know their cholesterol levels, many did not know the difference between LDL and HDL cholesterol levels. LDL, low-density lipoprotein, is the level of cholesterol that we should strive to keep down, with 30 to 50 being the ideal. HDL, high-density lipoprotein, is the "good-guy" cholesterol that we want to keep up, with 80 to 90 being the ideal (Rector-Page, 1992). The normal combined level is 140 to 165. However, the average American level is 210 (Rector-Page, 1992).

Many people fail to comprehend that cholesterol levels and heart problems go hand-in-hand. For every one percent reduction in over-all cholesterol levels, there is a two to four percent reduction in the risk of heart attacks (Cawood, 1993). As a matter of fact, heart disease is only a problem in countries where diets are high in cholesterol.

When you consider the American diet, it is no wonder that heart disease is such a problem. Consider a typical day: a dash through McDonald's for a sausage and biscuit with hash browns for breakfast; a quick lunch of a burger and fries; a moderate dinner of a grilled chicken salad, followed by a trip to Baskin-Robbins to reward ourselves for eating such a good meal. Not to mention the bag of chips and candy bar eaten for a snack somewhere in the day.

Cholesterol is a yellow, fatty material in the blood that looks a lot like a waxy substance. It can stick to the artery walls and harden into plaque, leading to heart disease.

In the well-known Framingham Heart Study, high levels of LDL and low levels of HDL cholesterol placed elderly men at greater risk of heart attack. After menopause, women with high LDL and low HDL levels were at greater risk for coronary problems (Cawood, 1993).

THE IMPACT OF FRUITS AND VEGETABLES ON CHOLESTEROL LEVELS

Clearly, macrobiotic diets and the intake of fruits and vegetables have a major impact on cholesterol levels. At the Harvard Medical School, 21 persons on macrobiotic diets had one serving of beef added to their diet daily for four weeks. After that month, their cholesterol levels were raised about 19 percent (Sacks et al., 1981).

We can improve our cholesterol levels by not only eliminating or moderating the intake of such foods as beef, but also by adding certain foods to our diets. For example, in one experimental project, men with high cholesterol levels were given pinto, navy or kidney beans to eat daily. Within three weeks, their cholesterol levels were reduced by an average of 20 percent (Anderson and Chen, 1982). For years, beans and legumes have been hailed as natural anti-cholesterol agents. "They are one of nature's cheapest, most widely available, fastest-acting and safest cholesterol-fighting drugs" (Carper, 1993, 46).

GARLIC AND CHOLESTEROL LEVELS

Garlic, once again, gets high marks in the fight against cholesterol. Whether cooked or raw, the equivalent of three cloves of garlic daily can reduce cholesterol by 10 to 15 percent (Bordia and Bansal, 1973). At a medical college in Bombay, India, 50 people were given three cloves of raw garlic daily. After just two months, their cholesterol levels dropped by at least 15 percent (Carper, 1993). Another study showed even higher results. In this two-month study, patients with high cholesterol were given the equivalent of 10 grams of garlic daily. Their cholesterol levels were reduced by an average of 28.5 percent (Augusti and Mathew, 1973).

ONIONS AND CHOLESTEROL LEVELS

Garlic's cousin, onion, is also full of phytochemicals that are effective in addressing cholesterol levels. Daily intake of onions raises HDL levels by 30 percent in most people with heart disease. Although cooked onions have benefit, the more they are cooked, they more they lose their potency to elevate HDL, the good-guy cholesterol (Carper, 1993).

AVOCADOS AND CHOLESTEROL LEVELS

Avocados are full of cholesterol-improving phytochemicals. "Although olive oil, almonds, and avocados are high in fat, most of it is monounsaturated fat and tends to improve cholesterol and dramatically protect rather than destroy arteries" (Carper, 1993, 53).

In a study in Israel, after three months of eating avocados, LDL levels were reduced by about 12 percent. In another study at the Wesley Medical Centre in Queensland, Australia, one group was put on a low fat diet to fight cholesterol, and the other group was put on a diet rich in avocados. The group on the low fat diet experienced a 4.9 percent reduction in cholesterol; however, the group on an avocado-rich diet experienced an astonishing 8.2 percent reduction in their cholesterol levels, with no other dietary modifications (Carper, 1993).

APPLES AND CHOLESTEROL LEVELS

Apples also share the limelight when it comes to cholesterol-reducing value. Pectin, a phytochemical found in apples, provides excellent fiber. In a French study, eating two apples a day for a month was shown to reduce cholesterol levels in 80 percent of the participants and by at least 10 percent in half of them. One person's cholesterol was reduced 30 percent (Carper, 1993).

These are not the only foods that have proven effective in reducing cholesterol. The following foods and their phytochemical components have also shown themselves as effective in the fight against cholesterol: vitamins C and E in strawberries, fiber in carrots, and galacturonic acid in grapefruit pulp.

Those of us with heart problems, or a family history of heart problems, must pay attention to our diet. "Remarkable new evidence shows that even if you ate recklessly in earlier days and even if you have already had heart problems, including a heart attack, changing your diet now may prevent future cardiac catastrophe and even halt or reverse arterial damage, helping restore arteries to health. It is not too early or too late" (Carper, 1993, 25). There's no time like the present to eat our way to a healthy heart!

12 Depression & Seasonal Affective Disorder (SAD)

"Depression is actually one of the early signs
of nutritional depletion."
—Richard Kunin

Depression is a state unwelcomed by most of us, yet most of us experience it at one time or another. Research indicates that we are ten times more likely to experience depression than our grandparents were (Seligman, 1991). In a survey conducted in 1991 by the *New York Times,* half of those interviewed stated that they themselves or a close family member had suffered with depression (*New York Times,* 1991).

According to the *Diagnostic and Statistic Manual of Mental Diagnosis* (1980), clinical depression is diagnosed when five of the eight following symptoms are described by a client: change in appetite and/or weight; change in sleeping patterns; change in activity levels; loss of interest and pleasure in activities; loss of energy and/or fatigue; feelings of guilt and/or worthlessness; loss of concentration; suicidal thoughts or feelings. Most people can readily identify with having experienced multiples of these symptoms at various times in their lives.

Depression is preventable and treatable in almost all cases. I have worked through the years with depressed people of all ages, of both genders, and of various levels of hope and hopelessness. In the mental health profession, it is often stated that we enter the field to resolve our own issues. Perhaps my own entrance into my graduate studies was in search of a nontraditional treatment for my own struggle with depression. Today I believe that there are various treatments for depression ranging anywhere from medication to psychotherapy to modifying food intake, or combinations of the three.

HOW FOOD AND DIET AFFECT OUR MOOD

Of all the areas that can be used to address depression and its symptoms, the one most often overlooked in my field is the effect of food or diet on our moods. In our "thin is in" society, dieting has a major impact on depression. One of the prime causes of depression among women is considered to be the starvation that results from fad and crash diets, which deplete our bodies of the calories and nutrients they need to keep us stable (Salaman and Scheer, 1994). Regardless of the media in the last several years, declaring: "DIETS DON'T WORK!" we continue to diet . . . "leading to nutritional deficiencies that put [us] at risk for future health problems" (McGrath, 1992, 274), one of them being depression.

When our bodies are depleted of necessary nutrients for long periods of time, depression is almost certainly guaranteed. "Chronic depression has been linked to a long-term subtle deficiency of certain nutrients that presumably can go unnoticed and uncorrected by the body for long periods" (Carper, 1993, 284).

Through the years of my studies, I have read everything from clinical research to self-help books regarding depression. However, it wasn't until recent years, when I began studying the concept of metabolic balancing, that I began to better understand the impact of food and diet on depression. After completing an extensive questionnaire, along with having some lab testing conducted, I discovered the great need my body has for fruits and vegetables. It then dawned on me that perhaps one factor contributing to my teenage and young adult depressions was the continual high protein, low carbohydrate diets I lived on, in an attempt to keep my weight down.

FRUITS AND VEGETABLES AFFECT LEVELS OF DEPRESSION

Out of curiosity, I began eating a steady diet of fruits and vegetables, getting most of my protein from vegetable sources. It was amazing how much more energetic, lively and happy I began to feel. Thus, my introduction to food and its impact on depression. I am not advocating that everyone follow my diet regimen, because I believe that the overall diet is an individual-specific matter. However, I do believe that there are some factors that we can all learn from, regarding diet and nutrition and their role in depression, anxiety and other mood disorders.

DEPRESSION: AN IMBALANCE OF NEUROTRANSMITTERS IN THE BRAIN

"Food and nutrition is a key factor in the brain's behavior and well-being. Poor diet is often the cause of depression" (Rector-Page, 1992, 194). A short biochemistry lesson might help emphasize the importance of food when determining its effect on depression. Biochemically, depression is described as an imbalance in the neurotransmitters in the brain. The neurotransmitters are the chemicals which relay messages between nerve cells in the brain. Depression can occur when there is a malfunction of these neurotransmitting chemicals.

Food has a definite effect on our neurotransmitters. One of those neurotransmitters that is affected by food and is significant in studying depression is serotonin. As levels of serotonin decrease, levels of depression seem to increase (McGrath, 1992, 315). In a study conducted by Dr. Young at the McGill University in Montreal in the Department of Psychiatry, it was found that depressed persons who either committed suicide or attempted suicide had decreased levels of serotonin (Young, 1991).

Potatoes contain a complex carbohydrate which fights against stress and anxiety by making way for more tryptophan, an amino acid, in the brain. It is then converted to serotonin (Carper, 1993), raising those serotonin levels that are so crucial to preventing and treating depression.

FOLIC ACID AND ITS EFFECT ON DEPRESSION

In other studies conducted by Dr. Young (1989), it was discovered that low levels of folic acid cause serotonin levels to drop. In an experimental study, patients were deprived of folic acid in their diets and were allowed none in supplemental form. Within five months, they reported sleeplessness, forgetfulness and irritability. When folic acid was reintroduced into their diet, their mood was restored to normal within two days.

Because it is evident that low levels of folic acid cause depression, one thing we can do is to make sure we supplement our diets with folic acid. Some of the foods that contain folic acid are: alfalfa, endive, chickpeas (garbanzo beans), lentils, split peas, whole wheat, brown rice, asparagus, green peas, collard greens, spinach and corn (*The Practical Encyclopedia of Natural Healing*, 1983).

ENDORPHIN LEVELS AND DEPRESSION

Endorphins are other chemicals in the brain made of amino acids, which are often studied in connection to depression. They are sometimes referred to as a "natural anesthetic," or are said to produce a "natural high." One of the keys to increasing endorphin levels for the relief of, treatment of or prevention of depression is exercise. One study compared the endorphin levels of joggers to sedentary men. Those who were sedentary reported more depression and greater stress levels. In addition, they had more stress hormones present in their blood, and their endorphin levels were lower than the joggers (Lobstein et al., 1983). So, once again, the importance of exercise is before us. The natural key to keeping endorphin levels up and depression down is regular exercise.

CHILI PEPPERS AS ANTIDEPRESSANTS

Have you ever craved Mexican food when you were depressed? I know that, in my 20s, although I didn't understand how or why, it became my first clue that a depression was setting in. I loved Mexican food then, and I love it now. But in those days, it wasn't a matter of loving it . . . it wasn't even a matter of being hungry. It was a matter of having to have it! Then when I began my practice, I saw variations of the same thing in many of my clients again and again. It was not until recent years, when some of the new research on phytochemicals began to emerge, that it began to make sense.

There is actually a phytochemical in chili peppers, known as capsaicin. The phytochemical burns the nerve ending in the tongue, sending a false alarm to the brain about a burn. The neurotransmitters in the brain respond to protect the body by sending out its chemical pain-killers, endorphins. The endorphins are then dumped into the blood, giving the body a "natural rush," or a "natural high." So maybe a trip to your favorite Mexican food restaurant is in order when you are depressed.

VITAMIN C AND DEPRESSION

Another critical consideration with food and depression is an ample intake of vitamin C. In a study over a six-week period, all patients deprived of vitamin C in their diet fell into a depressed state (Kunin, 1981). Vitamin C can be obtained from all the citrus fruits and fruit juices.

GARLIC AND DEPRESSION

Garlic is another food which contains phytochemicals that provide a boost in mood. In a test studying the benefits of garlic in treating cholesterol at the University of Hanover in Germany, there was a surprise element. When interviewing the patients who had received garlic to treat their cholesterol, it was also found that they reported feeling "less fatigue, anxiety, sensitivity, agitation and irritability" (Carper, 1993, 291).

ONIONS AS ANTIANXIETY AGENTS

As for the anxiety that many times can accompany depression and the sleeplessness which can be one symptom of depression, yellow and red onions might be the perfect "medicine." Quercetin, a phytochemical in yellow and red onions, works as a mild sedative on the central nervous system. In one French study, quercetin made mice quite drowsy (Carper, 1993).

AMINO ACIDS AS ANTIDEPRESSANTS

Many depressed people prefer not to take antidepressant medication. There are antidepressant medications which can be quite helpful. But for those people who are resistant to medication, many find taking natural amino acids, which can be obtained from health food stores, are helpful (Kirschman and Dunne, 1984). L-phenylalanine and L-tyrosine are the two most often recommended, with 500 mg. tablets of each being taken before the morning and the evening meals.

AVOID TAP WATER TO AVOID DEPRESSION

Another natural preventive for depression is drinking bottled water as opposed to tap water. There are so many treatment additives and chemicals added to the water coming into our homes and offices through the tap that we really have no idea what we are drinking. There are numerous studies which indicate that the chemicals used in treated water affect the neurotransmitter balances in the brain, which is a major cause of depression (Rector-Page, 1992). It has been a popular recommendation for years to drink eight glasses of water daily. It is my belief that eight glasses of tap water might do more damage than good. Drink bottled and/or filtered water, then go for eight!

EXERCISE, SEROTONIN AND DEPRESSION

The most natural treatment and preventive for depression is exercise. It is a well-researched fact that exercise produces endorphins. And when endorphin levels are increased, depression lifts (Whitaker,1995).

Remember that diet plays a major role in your disposition. Eating five serving of fruits and vegetables daily and six servings of grain is highly recommended. "A diet high in complex carbohydrates (vegetables and grains) raises serotonin levels and promotes emotional stability. Low levels of this brain neurotransmitter make you feel out of sorts and depressed" (Copeland, 1994, 79).

There is no denying that what we eat affects our mood. "There is no scientific dispute anymore that what you eat can affect your mood—whether you feel up or down. Although your food choices may seem based on taste or other conscious criteria, there's evidence that people often make unconscious food choices that change brain chemistry and put them in a better mood. They unwittingly 'self-medicate' with food antidepressants" (Carper, 1993, 284). This can be a blessing if it leads us to make healthy food choices. However, for some, this "self-medication" process gives rise to eating disorders which require special recovery processes.

SEASONAL AFFECTIVE DISORDER

Seasonal Affective Disorder (SAD) affects at least 35 million Americans (Goode, 1990). SAD traditionally occurs during the winter months when the shorter days have less sunlight. Typical symptoms include such things as unexplained depression, mood swings, unusual sleepiness, poor sleep, fatigue, craving of carbohydrates, an increase in appetite and weight gain.

SAD occurs four times more often in men than in women. In studying the symptoms of patients in geographical areas, it is interesting to note that only 1.4 percent of the residents of Florida polled experienced the symptoms of SAD. In New Hampshire, 10 percent reported experiencing the symptoms, and in Alaska, nine percent reported experiencing the symptoms of SAD (Cawood, 1993). This certainly concurs with the theory that the symptoms of SAD are associated with day length, since the time the sun is out daily in Florida exceeds the sunlight in New Hampshire or Alaska on most any given day.

SAD is reported to be the result of the pineal gland not getting enough stimulation from light. When this occurs, there is an overproduction of melatonin, a hormone secreted by the pineal gland. Ten times more melatonin is produced during the night than during daylight hours (Glanze, 1990).

Dr. Norman Rosenthal at the National Institute of Mental Health is a noted expert on the diagnosis and treatment of SAD. His primary method of treating SAD is relatively inexpensive. He recommends treatment with a "light box," a box containing lighting which is at least five times brighter than normal indoor lighting. He reported an 80 percent successful response rate when treating SAD patients with these lights (Rosenthal, 1984).

Dr. Rosenthal also understands the importance of carbohydrates to persons affected by SAD. He stated that carbohydrate cravings occur because carbohydrates are like antidepressants to the person with SAD. The carbohydrates boost the serotonin levels. In an experimental study, he gave cookies to SAD patients and nondepressed patients. In two hours, the nondepressed group reported feeling "zonked." However, the SAD patients reported feeling energetic, less depressed and less fatigued. Truly, carbohydrates affect people with SAD differently than they do those who are not depressed.

Diet, therefore, is an important consideration when considering treatment for SAD. "Conscious diet improvement is the main key in reducing SAD symptoms" (Rector-Page, 1992, 306). The best dietary relief for SAD is in eating dried beans, pasta, fruits and vegetables.

PREVENTING DEPRESSION, ANXIETY AND STRESS

Depression, anxiety and stress are rampant in our nation. I believe in the therapy process to help those in distress; I believe in medication to help those in severe distress. However, this is another area where prevention is the best policy. Extra helpings of fruits and vegetables daily, or supplements containing their extracts, might provide relief to some struggling with mood disorders. Before cycling further into depression, or before taking antidepressants, try a diet rich in carbohydrates from fruits and vegetables. And try a moderate, regular exercise program. You have nothing to lose but "the blues."

13 Antioxidants vs. Free Radicals: The Battle Fruits & Vegetables Can Win

"Nothing protects your health and extends life more than a steady supply of antioxidants to your cells."
— Jean Carper, 1993

In almost every type of publication you pick up now, from health newsletters to popular ladies magazines, you see articles about antioxidants and free radicals. A friend of mine, who is a physical therapist, wished me "good luck" if I tried to read everything out there about the subject to include it in my book. I'm sure it would take more than "good luck" to complete such a task; I think it would be several volumes of books. Therefore, I intend to give only the most basic of explanations of the whole antioxidant versus free radical movement, in order for you to understand the winning power of fruits and vegetables and their phytochemicals in this war.

WHAT ARE FREE RADICALS?

Molecules are the building blocks that make up cells and hold all the cells together. The cells make up our bodies, our body parts and our organs. The molecules are held together by electrons. Each molecule has pairs of electrons which keep it in perfect balance. When something happens and the molecule ends up with one less electron than normal, it becomes imbalanced, making it lopsided and unstable, much like a "goofy ball." A "goofy ball" (if you haven't been in a toy store lately) is like a small beach ball blown up, with a weight attached inside the ball at one side. The weight causes the ball to roll and fly, when thrown, in a totally goofy, out-of-control manner. Molecularly, this is a free radical.

However, this "goofy ball" type of molecule isn't happy alone. Misery loves company. Once flailing through the system, it begins to bump other molecules, stealing their electrons. However, this does not fix the one free radical; hence, now we have two free radicals. The multiplication, snow-ball effect is thus underway.

FREE RADICALS AS "GOOD GUYS"

The presence of some free radicals in our bodies is necessary and helpful. They can destroy bacteria and viruses, produce energy, fight off infections, assist in the production of hormones and control the tone of our "smooth muscles," which help in regulation of our internal organs.

It is when these free radicals are in the overproduction mode in our bodies that we get in trouble. They can then begin their destructive process of damaging healthy tissue. Dr. Kenneth H. Cooper of the Cooper Aerobics Center in Dallas, Texas, stated that "free radicals pose one of the greatest single threats to our public health as we approach the brave, new world of the twenty-first century" (Cooper, 1994, 8).

WHERE DO FREE RADICALS COME FROM?

Where do these free radicals, which pose such a great threat, come from? They are produced in our bodies, but they also come in from the environment. The list of causes of free radicals could go on for pages. Some of the basic causes are as follows: over-strenuous exercise, illness, some prescription medications, cigarette smoke, air pollution, herbicides, pesticides, ultraviolet lighting, alcohol and fried foods.

As you can see, free radicals can be produced in our bodies or come in from the outside. But no matter where they come from, once inside in an abundant number, their forces are at work. They bond with cell parts and begin to destroy anything with which they bond. This is called the "oxidative process." Scientists have linked this oxidation process to over 60 chronic diseases, as well as to the aging process itself (Carper, 1993). Some of those diseases which we are familiar with are cancer, heart disease, premature aging, cataracts, AIDS, ulcerative colitis, Parkinson's disease, sickle cell disease, leukemia, high blood pressure, strokes, asthma, pancreatitis, diverticulitis, peptic ulcers, rheumatoid arthritis and early senility.

"Many researchers are convinced that the cumulative effects of free radicals also underlie the gradual deterioration that is the hallmark of aging in all individuals, healthy as well as sick" (*Health Horizons*, Spring 1995). Understanding the power of these free radicals, how they effect the aging process and the devastation they leave in their paths within our bodies has revolutionized the manner in which scientists, researchers and doctors are studying, addressing, and treating disease.

WHAT ARE ANTIOXIDANTS?

When our body notes that there are too many free radicals roaming through our bodies, doing their destructive work, it sends out scavengers to hunt them down and devour them. These scavengers are called antioxidants. "Numerous studies have revealed that antioxidants can provide very significant protection against harmful cell damage by neutralizing free radicals" (*Health Horizons*, Spring 1995).

The benefits of antioxidants in fighting disease and restoring our bodies to optimal health are phenomenal. Most of the damage that free radicals do can be prevented by antioxidants, and some of that damage can be treated by antioxidants. For example, free radicals cause our LDL cholesterol to turn into plaque, blocking arteries, which can cause various coronary problems, and they can also attack the cell's genetic coding, which can lead to cancer. Antioxidants can prevent such blocking and mutations and can actually "un-do" some of the damage.

Antioxidants have proven to be helpful in the prevention and treatment of many diseases and maladies. Following is a summary of some of the research.

ATHEROSCLEROSIS

Atherosclerosis occurs when plaque builds up inside our blood vessels, of course blocking the flow of our blood. Although we normally, and rightfully so, blame this process on high LDL cholesterol in the blood, research has indicated that only when the cholesterol has been damaged, or oxidized by free radicals, is the risk of heart disease increased.

Studies have shown the plaque found in vessels is high in "oxidized" cholesterol, which is cholesterol that has been invaded and damaged by free radicals (Lin, 1993). In the late 1980s and early 1990s, the Scottish Heart Health Study compared the differences in levels of atherosclerosis in people with diets high in antioxidants with people consuming lesser amounts. The study revealed that the men with high antioxidant intake were at significantly lower risk of heart disease (Cooper, 1994).

HEART DISEASE

The plaque buildup of atherosclerosis, caused by free radicals, can limit the blood supply to the heart. The blood is the vehicle that transports the oxygen and nutrients to the heart. The heart must have the oxygen and nutrients to thrive and function. When this supply is limited, the heart may develop painful symptoms, such as angina pectoris. This is the body's way of warning us that tissue damage may be happening in our heart. If ignored, a heart attack can occur. This is an example of the domino, snow ball effect of free radicals in our bodies.

Studies conducted on the East coast have found that antioxidants have a major protective role against heart disease. In one group, there was a 50 percent reduction in heart attacks in men when antioxidants were consumed. In another study, the risk of heart disease for both men and women was significantly reduced when diets were high in antioxidants (Cooper, 1994).

CANCER

In the simplest definition, "cancer is the uncontrolled growth and multiplication of [unhealthy] cells, resulting in their consuming all available nutrients until healthy cells are starved to death" (Lin, 1993, 26). There is much research about the function of free radicals in the development of cancer. A simplified statement to summarize much of the research would be that the free radicals override the gene's normal instructions to stop growing and multiplying when there is a problem. When cancer begins, the body's natural response is to send out a line of defense to surround and contain the cancer. Researchers believe that free radicals destroy this surrounding protective barrier, allowing the mass to continue to grow despite the body's attempt to stop it.

Antioxidants play a major role in the prevention of such a process. One study at the Johns Hopkins University found that high levels of antioxidants in the blood were indicators of lower incidences of cancer (Menkes et al., 1986). Also, in a study conducted in Finland, it was found that people with lung cancer who were given antioxidant treatments along with chemotherapy had longer survival times (Cooper, 1994).

Once again, a good defense is the best offense. But there is further hope. Antioxidants are not only a good defense or preventive, they are also effective in the treatment of cancer. "Already, the use of free radical fighter nutrients, or antioxidants, has been found to alleviate many of the toxic side effects that usually occur during chemotherapy. As is true for most things, prevention is better than cure; antioxidants may help substantially reduce the risk of developing cancer in the first place, as well as other degenerative diseases" (Lin, 1993, 28).

AIDS

Free radicals are definitely an enemy to those diagnosed with the AIDS virus. The presence of free radicals may actually weaken the membranes of cells, allowing easier entrance of the virus into the T-cells. Free radicals also multiply exponentially when the virus is present, depleting the body of the immune system response it might normally have to fight bacterial and viral infections. In addition, some drugs which are used to treat AIDS actually generate free radicals. Research has indicated that using antioxidant treatments in conjunction with some of the traditional treatments actually reduces toxic responses and may help stimulate the immune systems of AIDS patients (Lin, 1993).

CATARACTS

Ultraviolet light, as mentioned earlier, can actually generate free radicals. When this kind of light enters our eyes, it can actually produce free radicals in our tender eye tissue. When this occurs, damaged proteins in the lenses of our eyes produce opaque masses, known as cataracts. Interestingly, the fluid in our eyes contains some of the highest concentrations of antioxidants found in our bodies. High intake of antioxidants play a major role in the prevention of cataracts. At the University of Western Ontario, it was found that those patients who were free of cataracts consumed significantly greater amounts of antioxidants than those who had cataracts (Robertson et al., 1991). At the University of Maryland School of Medicine, researchers concluded that some of the damage caused by free radicals could be thwarted by increased intake of antioxidants (Varma, 1991).

ARTHRITIS

One type of arthritis occurs when the fluid sac (the synovial sac) in the joint is destroyed, no longer providing cushion in the joint area. Free radicals may actually destroy the outer lining of the sac, causing the fluid to leak out. Because this leaves no support to the bones, the area can develop inflammation, which, through a chain of events, actually produces more free radicals. The intake of antioxidants can halt the progression of free radical production, possibly retarding or stopping the progression of arthritis altogether (Werbach, 1993).

PARKINSON'S DISEASE

Parkinson's is a neurological disease, with tremoring, rigidity, and loss of reflex being the most predominant symptoms. The exact cause of this disease is not fully understood. But once again, researchers believe that free radicals could play a role. It is believed that the brain somehow produces toxic compounds such as free radicals which begin a progression of damage to the central nervous system.

There is research supporting the notion that antioxidants may not only protect against Parkinson's (Stern, 1987), but that they may also delay the progression of the disease once it is diagnosed. One study conducted at the Neurological Institute of New York and the Columbia University College of Physicians and Surgeons worked with patients with early Parkinson's disease. They were administered high doses of antioxidants, delaying the normal medication given to those diagnosed with the disease for two and a half years past those who were not taking increased antioxidants (Fahn, 1991). This suggests that antioxidants may actually slow the progression of the disease.

WHY SHOULD WE TAKE ANTIOXIDANTS?

This is certainly not an exhaustive list of the diseases that free radicals can cause or what antioxidants can do in the areas of prevention, protection, and treatment. But the bottomline is the same, whether the list be limited to those listed above, or whether it be inclusive of all 60 related diseases: "Antioxidants can prevent or delay the onset of many health problems, including cancer and heart disease" (Cooper, 1994, xii).

"One of the great revelations of the last few years, according to a massive and growing body of evidence, is that you may be able to eat your way out of this dilemma, insofar as the boundaries of human life span and genetics allow. You can supply your cells with antioxidant food compounds that strike down, intercept and extinguish rampaging oxygen molecules, and even repair some of their damage. Foods, notably plant food — fruits and vegetables — are packed with a variety of ferocious antioxidants" (Carper, 1993, 9).

WHAT FOODS CONTAIN ANTIOXIDANTS?

The list of foods high in antioxidants is quite lengthy. Some of the more common foods we consume that are high in antioxidants are avocados, asparagus, berries, broccoli, Brussels sprouts, cabbage, carrots, chili peppers, collard greens, garlic, kale, lettuce, onions (yellow and red), oranges, pepper, pink grapefruit, pumpkin, red grapes, spinach, sweet potatoes, tomatoes and watermelon.

Vitamins C and E, beta carotene and selenium are the antioxidants most noted for their free radical prevention in the body (Whitaker, 1995). In addition to finding antioxidants in the foods listed above, they can also be bought as supplements. Different experts recommend different doses, so you will want to check with your doctor before beginning your antioxidant program. Dr. Kenneth Cooper, of the Cooper Aerobics Center in Dallas, Texas, recommends an "antioxidant cocktail" be taken daily. He recommends the following daily intake (see following page):

The Facts About Phytochemicals

VITAMIN E

400 IU*	Ages 21-50
600 IU*	Ages 51 +

VITAMIN C

1,000 mg	Women
1,500 mg	Men — Ages 21 - 50
2,000 mg	Men — Ages 51 +

BETA CAROTENE

25,000 IU*	Ages 22 - 50
50,000 IU	Ages 51 +

* An IU is an International Unit and is equivalent to approximately one milligram.

Dr. Julian Whitaker, of the Whitaker Wellness Institute, Inc., in Newport Beach, California, recommends the following antioxidant supplementation for optimal health benefits (Whitaker, 1995):.

Vitamin E	400-800 IU
Vitamin C	100 - 250 mg
Beta carotene	5,000 - 25,000 IU
Selenium	100-200 mcg (micrograms)

The benefits of antioxidants are evident. However, the benefits are definitely not limited to those reported in this chapter. They actually encompass all the studies and their results contained in this entire book, because our primary source of antioxidants, whether taken in supplemental form or through our food intake, is fruits and vegetables. If we are to win the battle for our health, increasing our intake of antioxidants is a wise step in planning our victory. "Lower intensity exercise, antioxidant supplements and the right kind of diet can strengthen your free radical defenses significantly" (Cooper, 1994, 171).

14 A Prescription for a Healthy, Happy Life

> "Live your life as most people
> do and you
> will be forced to settle
> for what most people settle for."
> — Charles Givens, 1993

The quality of our lives is primarily in our hands. The evidence of what we need to do to promote our health, prevent disease, and win the battle of disease versus health is within the covers of this book. I challenge you to consider taking charge!

In my professional field, a new buzz word emerged several years ago: "self-care." Many people rejected the notion, believing that it was selfish. Even the great teacher, Jesus, supported the notion. When teaching the people of his time, he offered a great piece of advice that would serve us well today: "Love your neighbor as yourself." Think about it. Those who are self-serving would be serving of their neighbors if they took in this piece of wisdom. Those who were nicer to their neighbors than they were to themselves would learn more about self-love. Self-care is definitely the summary word for all the seven prescriptions I'd like to present to each of you for a happy, healthy life.

RX #1: CHOOSE WELLNESS AS A WAY OF LIFE

Wellness has many definitions, but I use the word to denote the choice of living a life of active prevention, rather than stumbling through life, depending on treatment for disease and problems. My prescription is actually a wake-up call. PAY ATTENTION . . . to your life, to your health, to the health of those you love. Dr. Julian Whitaker (1995) also strongly recommends a lifestyle of "wellness." According to his definition, this lifestyle involves taking responsibility for your health; having a positive mental outlook; eating nutritiously; maintaining ideal body weight; developing a healthy heart with proper diet and physical activity; having high energy levels; learning to handle stress and challenges optimally; balancing life stress with rest and recreation and stopping the use of alcohol, tobacco, and/or illegal drugs. I certainly have no argument with his recommendations for wellness.

RX #2: HAVE FUN! AND LAUGH!

I love the little phrase that became popular several years ago: "Are we having fun yet?" For too many people, the answer is no. Fun, or recreation, does just exactly what it says. Recreation actually re-creates us at a spiritual level. Yet fun has virtually become a thing of the past for many individuals and families. "Many Americans will have to relearn the art of having fun . . . an activity that was largely shoved aside in the last two decades" (*Healing Unlimited*, 1994, 421). Even if we have to relearn the art, it is definitely an art worth pursuing.

An old proverb (Proverbs 17:22) states that a "cheerful heart is good medicine." So in the process of rediscovering fun . . . laugh! Dr. Norman Cousins has done a tremendous amount of research about the healing power of laughter. Dr. William Fry, a professor of psychiatry at Stanford University, in an article in *American Health*, stated that laughter could aid in digestion, lower blood pressure, stimulate the heart, activate our right brain, strengthen our muscles, soothe arthritic pain and keep us alert!

RX #3: EXERCISE MODERATELY AND REGULARLY

Dr. Julian Whitaker says: "If the physiological benefits of physical activity could be put in a pill, you would have the most powerful anti-aging and health-promoting medication available" (Whitaker, 1995, p. 31). The benefits of getting and staying active are in practically every newspaper and magazine we read. Yet we often come equipped with thousands of reasons why we don't . . . or can't . . . or will get started when . . . Get up right now and walk through your home briskly, or do some toe-touches. There is no time like the present. And let me tell you . . . the Good Fairy isn't coming to do it for you! You will feel better, you will look better and you will be healthier!

RX #4: GET ADEQUATE REST

Many of us have incredibly busy, hectic lives. Whether you are busy watching TV, shuttling your kids, writing a report, studying for school, working overtime or doing that last load of laundry, you probably have a busy lifestyle. We live in a time when we have become "human doings" more than "human beings." Remember the cute little saying of the 1970's and 1980's?. . . "Take time to smell the roses." This is an excellent prescription. We can all get by with inadequate rest for awhile, but the long-term effects are disastrous. Make time to rest, relax and get adequate sleep. You will be surprised how much better you will feel. And those around you may like you better too!

RX #5: GET YOUR SPIRITUAL LIFE IN ORDER

Don't worry. I'm not here to evangelize, proselytize, nor convert you. I simply know that even research points out that people who practice spirituality have better health. In a recent study conducted by a psychologist at Purdue University, it was found that twice as many people who did not practice spirituality had health problems than those who practiced spirituality. In addition, 36 percent of those who attended some sort of religious meetings weekly reported excellent health, while only 26 percent of nonattendees did (Ferraro and Albrecht-Jensen, 1991).

RX #6: GO AN EXTRA MILE

Og Mandino, one of my favorite authors, in his classic book, *The Greatest Miracle in the World*, beautifully encourages the extra mile in the "memo from God."

Now I give you the law of success in every venture. Many centuries ago this law was given to your forefathers from a mountain top. Some heeded the law and lo, their life was filled with the fruit of happiness, accomplishment, gold, and peace of mind. Most listened not, for they sought magic means, devious routes, or waited for the devil called luck to deliver to them the riches of life. They waited in vain . . . just as you waited, and then they wept, as you wept, blam-

ing their lack of fortune on my will.

The law is simple. Young or old, pauper or king, white or black, male or female . . . all can use the secret to their advantage; for of all rules and speeches and scriptures of success and how to attain it only one method has never failed . . . whomsoever shall compel ye to go with him one mile . . . go with him two.

This then is the law . . . The secret that will produce riches and acclaim beyond your dreams. Go another mile!

(Mandino, 1975, p. 99).

Can you even imagine what a wonderful place to live this world would be if we each went the extra mile? Try it . . . today . . . the promised result is success and happiness!

RX #7: INCREASE YOUR INTAKE OF FRUITS AND VEGETABLES (IMPROVE YOUR DIET AND INTAKE OF SUPPLEMENTS)

The benefits of fruits and vegetables have been undeniably proven within the covers of this book. Increase your intake to the recommended servings daily. In addition, read the Appendix at the end of the book that tells you where you can buy supplements which contain the phytochemicals of fruits and vegetables.

Review your diet. Reduce your intake of fat and increase your intake of fruits, vegetables and other fibers. There are many supplements on the market that might be helpful to you. In my first book, *Bountiful Health, Boundless Energy, and Brilliant Youth: The Facts about DHEA*, I have outlined the astounding benefits of taking Dioscorea, a precursor of DHEA. In my second book, *The Miracle in Aloe Vera: The Facts about Polymannans*, I have reported how scientific research has proven the benefits of Aloe vera to be more than an old wives' tale. Read these and other books that promote health and recommend natural healing methods.

You don't have to be a "health food nut" to get the benefits of a good diet. Increasing your intake of fruits and vegetables, even if you don't modify your "junk food habit" can have a great pay-off . . . the pay-off is life, a healthy life!

I like to end my workshops informing my participants that we have many choices in life. We can choose to learn, or choose to remain ignorant. We can choose to care about those around us, or choose to be alone. We can choose to eat wisely or choose the wrong foods. We can choose to drive to the corner grocery store, or choose to walk. There are so many choices. But in all your choices, above all . . . PLEASE CHOOSE LIFE!

BIBLIOGRAPHY

Adams, Rex. *Miracle Medicine Foods.* West Nyack, NY: Parker Publishing Co. Inc., 1977.

Airola, Paavo. *Are You Confused?* Sherwood, Oregon: Health Plus Publishers, 1991.

Alabaster, Oliver, "Effect of Beta Carotene and Wheat Bran Fiber on Colonic Aberrant Crypt and Tumor Formation in Rats Exposed to Azoxymethane and High Dietary Fat." *Carcinogenesis.* Vol 16, No 1, January 1995, 127-132.

American Cancer Society. *Eat to Learn, Learn to Eat: The Link Between Nutrition and Learning.* Wahington, DC: National Health/Education Consortium, 1993.

The American Heart Association Heart Book. New York: Dutton, 1980.

American Institute for Cancer Research Newsletter. "AICR Diet and Cancer Project: A Global Perspective on Good Health." Vol 49, Fall 1995, 4-5.

American Institute for Cancer Research Newsletter. "Garlic May Offer More Than Flavor: Research Shows Cancer-Suppressing Potential." Vol 48, Summer 1995, 10.

American Journal of Nursing. "America's Getting Fatter." September 1994, 9.

Anderson, J.W. and W.L. Chen. "Effects of Legumes and Their Soluble Fibers on Cholesterol-Rich Lipoproteins." *American Chemical Society Abstracts AGFD.* Vol 39, 1982.

Auer, W., A. Eiber, E. Kertkorn. "Hypertension and Hyperlipidaemia: Garlic helps in Mild Cases." *British Journal Clinical Practice.* Vol 44 (Supplement 69), 1990, 3-7.

Augusti, K.T. and P.T. Mathew. "Lipid Lowering Effect of Allicin on Long Term Feeding to Normal Rats." *Experientia.* Vol 30, No 5, 1973, 468-470.

Baranowski, T., S. Domel, and R. Gould. "Increasing Fruit and Vegetable Consumption Among Fourth and Fifth Grade Students from Focus Groups Using Reciprocal Determinism." *J. Nutr. Education.* Vol 25, No 3, 1993, 114-120.

Barona, F.E. and M.R. Tansey. "Isolation, Purification, Identification, Synthesis of Activity of the Anticandidal Compounds of Allium sativum, and a Hypothesis for Its Mode of Action. *Mycologia.* Vol 69, 1977, 793-824.

Barrett-Carmen, Elizabeth and K.T. Khaw. *American Journal of Clinical Nutrition.* Vol 39, 1984, 963-968.

Barrie, S.A., J.V. Wright, and J.E. Pizzarno. "Effects of Garlic Oil on Platelet Aggregation, Serum Lipids, and Blood Pressure." *J Orthomol Med.* Vol 2, 1987, 15-21.

Begley, Sharon. "Beyond Vitamins." *Newsweek.* April 25, 1994, 45-49.

Better Nutrition for Today's Living. "Veggie Corner: Garlic Is an Herb that Boosts Health, Immunity." Vol 57, No 3, March 1995, 16.

Better Nutrition for Today's Living. "Vitamin Update: Vitamin D Slows Breast, Colon, Prostate Cancer." Vol 57, No 3, March 1995, 20.

Better Nutrition for Today's Living. "Veggie Corner: Garlic Has Numerous Medicinal Qualities." May 1995, 18-20.

Better Nutrition for Today's Living. "Health Watch: Bran and Beta Carotene May Check Colon Cancer." May 1995, 12.

Block, G., and S.M. Menkes. "Ascorbic Acid in Cancer Prevention." In *Nutrition and Cancer Prevention: Investigating the Role of Micronutrients.* Edited by T.E. Moon and M.S. Micozzi. New York: Marcel Decker, Inc., 1988.

Blossom H., M.A. Patterson, G. Block, W. Rosenberger, D. Pee, and L. Kahle. "Fruits and Vegetables in the American Diet: Data for the NHANES II Survey." Vol 80, No 12, 1990, 1443-1449.

Bordia, A. "Effect of Garlic on Blood Lipids in Patients with Coronary Heart Disease." *American Journal of Clinical Nutrition.* Vol 7, No 3, 1981, 2100-2103.

Bordia, A. and H.C. Bansal. "Essential Oil of Garlic in Prevention of Atherosclerosis." *The Lancet.* Vol 11, 1973, 1491.

Bordia, A., H.C. Bansal, S. Arara, and S.V. Singh. "Effect of the Essential Oils of Garlic and Onion on Alimentary Hyperlipemia." *Atherosclerosis.* Vol 21, 1975, 15-19.

Bordia, A. S.K. Verma, and A.K. Vyas. "Effect of Essential Oil of Onion and Garlic on Experimental Atherosclerosis in Rabbits." *Atherosclerosis.* Vol 26, 1977, 379-386.

Boston Globe. "Type of Vitamin A May Reduce Heart Ills." November 14, 1990.

Bibliography

Boston Globe. "Very Low Rate of Fat in Diet Is Advised to Fight Cancer." April 23, 1991.

Burghart, J. and B. Devany. *The School Nutrition Dietary Assessment Study: Summary of Findings.* Washington, DC: Mathematica Policy Research, Inc. and U.S. Department of Agriculture, 1993.

Byers, T.E., S. Graham, B. P. Haughey, J. R. Marshall, and M.K. Swanson. "Diets and Lung Cancer Risk: Findings from the Western New York Diets Study." *American Journal of Epidemiology.* Vol 125, 1987, 351-363.

Byers, Tim, Paul A. LaChance, and Herbert F. Pierson. "New Directions: The Diet-Cancer Link." *Patient Care.* November 20, 1990, 34-48.

Carper, Jean. *Food — Your Miracle Medicine.* New York: Harper Collins Publisher, 1993.

Cavallito, C.J. and J.H. Bailey. "Allicin, the Antibacterial Principle of Allium Sativum. I. Isolation, Physical Properties and Antibacterial Action." *Journal of the American Chemical Society.* Vol 66, 1945, 1950-1951.

Cavallito, C.J., J.H. Bailey, and J.S. Buck. "The Antibacterial Principle of Allium Sativum. III. Its Precursor and Essential Oil of Garlic." *Journal of the American Chemical Society.* Vol 67, 1945, 1032-1033.

Cawood, Frank W. and Associates. *Proven Home Remedies and Natural Healing Secrets.* Peachtree City, GA: FC &A Publishing, 1995.

Centers for Disease Control. "Selected Tobacco-Use and Dietary Patterns Among High School Students." *MMWR.* Vol 41, no 24, 1991, 417-421.

Chopra, Deepak. *Ageless Body, Timeless Mind.* New York: Harmony Books, 1993.

Clandinin, D.R. and A.R. Robblee. "Rapeseed Meal in Animal Nutrition." *Journal of the American Oil Chemical Society.* Vol 58, 1981, 682-686.

Consumer Reports on Health. "How Am I Supposed to Eat All Those Fruits and Vegetables?" Vol 5, No 1, January 1993, 4-5.

Consumer Reports on Health. "Nutrition Update: A Cornucopia of Cancer Fighters." Vol 7, No 2, February 1995, 21.

Consumer Reports on Health. "Nutrition Update: Produce in a Pill?" Vol 7, No 4, April 1995, 39.

Consumer Reports on Health. "Overview." Vol 7, No 4, April 1995, 45.

Consumer Reports on Health. "No More Meat?" Vol 7, No 10, October 1995, 109-110, 112.

Cooper, Kenneth H. *Antioxidant Revolution.* Nashville: Thomas Nelson Publishers, 1994.

Copeland, Mary Ellen. *Living Without Depression and Manic Depression.* Oakland, CA: New Harbinger Books, Inc., 1994.

Corrieri, Donna. "Cabbage Leaves: An Effective Treatment for Swollen Tissues." *Journal of Human Lactation.* Vol 8, No 3, 1992, 126-127.

Cotugna, Nancy and Connie E. Vickery. "Development and Supermarket Field Testing of Videotaped Nutrition Messages for Cancer Risk Reduction." *Public Health Reports.* Vol 107, No 6, November-December 1992, 691-694.

Crabb, Charlene. "Power Plants." *Men's Fitness.* February 1995, 38-41.

Crayhon, Robert. *Robert Crayhon's Nutrition Made Simple.* New York, M. Evans and Co., Inc., 1994.

De Schepper, Luc. *Human Condition: Critical.* Santa Fe, New Mexico: Full of Life Publishing, 1993.

Diagnostic and Statistic Manual of Mental Diagnosis, Third Edition. American Psychiatric Association, Washington, 1980.

Doll, R. and R. Peto. "The Causes of Cancer: Quantitative Estimates of Avoidable Risk of Cancer in the United States Today." *Journal of the National Cancer Institute.* Vol 66, 1981, 1192-1308.

Faelten, Sharon. *The Complete Book of Minerals for Health.* Emmaus, PA: Rodale Books, 1981, 427-429.

Fahn, S. "An Open Trial of High-Dosage Antioxidants in Early Parkinson's Disease." *American Journal of Clinical Nutrition.* Vol 543, 1991, 380S-382S.

Feldman, David. "Vitamin D Slows Tumor Growth." *Medical Tribune.* September 22, 1994, 19.

Ferraro, K.F. and C.M. Albrecht-Jensen. "Does Religion Influence Health?" *Journal of Scientific Study Religion.* Vol 30, 1991, 193-203.

Fitzsimmons, Mary Lee and Liane Fales. "Colon Cancer Prevention Update." *Seminars in Oncology Nursing.* Vol 9, No 3, August, 1993, 163-168.

Food Guide Pyramid. Washington, DC: United States Department of Agriculture, Human Nutrition Information Services, 1992, Leaflet #572.

Fraser, Gary E., W. Lawrence Beeson, and Roland L. Phillips. "Diet and Lung Cancer in California Seventh-day Adventists." *American Journal of Epidemiology.* Vol 133, 1991, 683-693.

Bibliography

Friend, Tim. "Kids Who Shun Veggis Risk Ill Health Later." *USA Today.* March 29, 1995.

Givens, Charles. *Super Self: Doubling Your Personal Effectiveness.* New York, New York: Simon & Schuster, 1993.

Gladstar, Rosemary. *Herbal Healing for Women.* New York: Simon and Schuster, 1993.

Glanze, Walter, Ed. *Mosby's Medical Dictionary.* St. Louis: The C.V. Mosby Co., 1990.

Goode, E. "Mind Health: The Winter Blues." *Vogue.* February 1990, 230.

Gordon, Jay. "Take Ten Pounds of Cabbage and Call Me in the Morning." *Journal of Longevity Research.* Vol 1, No 2, December 1994, 32-34, 47.

Grunberg, N.E. "The Effects of Nicotine and Cigarette Smoking on Food Consumption and Taste Preferences." *Addictive Behavior.* Vol 7, 1982, 317-331.

Grunwald, J. "Garlic and Cardiovascular Risk Factors." *British Journal of Clinical Pharmacology.* Vol 29, 1990, 582.

Haenzel, W., F. B. Lake, and M. Segi. "A Case-Controlled Study of Large Bowel Cancer in Japan." *Journal National Cancer Inst.* Vol 64, 1980, 17-22.

Harder, Joan. "Defense Against Breast Cancer." *Bestways.* September 1986, 367.

Hathcock, John N. "Safety and Regulatory Issues for Phytochemical Sources: 'Designer Foods.'" *Nutrition Today.* November/December 1993, 23-25.

Healing Unlimited. New York, NY. Boardroom Classics, 1994

Health Horizons. "Researchers State Cruciferous Vegetables May Help Prevent Cancer." Spring 1993, 1-2.

Health Horizons. "What You Must Know about Anti-Oxidants and Cell Damaging Free Radicals." Spring 1995, 4-5.

Healthy Cell News. "Garlic: Folk Remedy Rediscovered." Spring/Summer 1995, 6.

Healthy People 2000: National Health Promotion and Disease Prevention Objectives. Washington, DC: U.S. Dept. of Health and Human Services, 1990, DHHS (PHS) Publication # 91-50212.

Heaney, Robert P. and Connie M. Weaver. "Calcium Absorption from Kale." *American Journal of Clinical Nutrition.* Vol 51, 1990, 656-657.

Heinerman, John. *Heinerman's Encyclopedia of Fruits, Vegetables and Herbs.* West Nyack, New York: Parker Publishing Company, 1988.

Hermann, Mindy. "The Healing Power of Fruits and Vegetables." *McCalls.* December 1994, 16-18.

Huddleson, I.F., J. DuFrain, K.C. Barrons, and M. Giefel. "Antibacterial Substances in Plants." *Journal of the American Veterinary Medical Association.* Vol 105, 1944, 394-397.

Hudson, J.B. and G.H.N. Towers. "Therapeutic Potential of Plant Photosensitizers." *Pharmac. Ther.* Vol 49, 1991, 181-222.

Hunan Medical College, China. "Garlic in Cryptococcal meningitis. A Preliminary Report of 21 Cases." *Chinese Medical Journal.* Vol 93, 1980, 123-126.

Illman, Deborah. "Selenium Compounds in Garlic, Onion Identified." *Chemical and Engineering News.* October 17, 1994, 53.

Jack, Alex, Editor. *Let Food Be Thy Medicine.* Becket, Ma: One Peaceful World, 1991.

Jain, R.C. "Onion and Garlic in Experimental Cholesterol Atherosclerosis in Rabbits: I. Effect on Serum Lipids and Development of Atherosclerosis." *Artery.* Vol 1, No 2, 1975, 115-125.

Jain, R.C. "Onion and Garlic in Experimental Cholesterol Induced Atherosclerosis." *Indian Journal of Medical Research.* Vol 64, No 10, 1976, 1509-1515.

Jain, R.C. and D.B. Konar. "Onion and Garlic in Experimental Cholesterol Atherosclerosis in Rabbits: II. Effect on Serum Lipids and Development of Atherosclerosis." *Artery.* Vol 2, No 6, 1976, 531-539.

Jezowa, L., T. Rafinski, and T. Wroncinski. "Investigations on the Antibiotic Activity of Allium Sativum I." *Herba Polonica.* Vol 12, 1966, 3.

Johnson, M.G. and R.H. Vaughn. "Death of Salmonella typhimurium and Escherichia coli in the Presence of Freshly Reconstituted Dehydrated Garlic and Onion." *Applied Microbiology.* Vol 17, 1969, 903-905.

Kamanna, V.S. and N. Chandrasekhara. "Effect of Garlic on Serum Lipoproteins and Lipoprotein Cholesterol Levels in Albino Rats Rendered Hypercholestermic by Feeding Cholesterol." *Lipids.* Vol 17, No 7, 1982, 483-488.

Bibliography

Kemper, Donald W., The Healthwise Staff, and Diana Stilwell, Editor. *Healthwise Handbook: A Self-Care Manual for You.* Boise, Idaho: Healthwise® Publication, 1990).

Kirschman, John D. and Lavon J. Dunne. *Nutrition Almanac.* New York, NY: McGraw Hill Book Co., 1984.

Kitts, David D. "Bioactive Substances in Food: Identification and Potential Uses." *Cancer Journal of Physiol. Pharmacol.* Vol 72, 1994, 423-434.

Kleijnen, J., P. Knipschild, and G.T. Riet. "Garlic, Onions, and Cardiovascular Risk Factors: A Review of the Evidence from Human Experiments with Emphasis on Commercially Available Preparations." *British Journal of Clinical Pharmacology.* Vol 28, 1989, 535-544.

Kolonel, L. N., J.H. Hankin, and C.N. Yoshizawa. "Vitamin A and Prostate Cancer in Elderly Men: Enhancement of Risk." *Cancer Research.* Vol 47, 1987, 2982-2983.

Kritchevsy, D. "Effect of Garlic Oil on Experimental Atherosclerosis in Rabbits." *Artery.* Vol 1, No 4, 1975, 319-323.

Krotkov, V.M. "The Action of Garlic Juice on Blood Pressure." *Vrachebnoe Deol.* Vol 6, 1966, 123.

Kunin, Richard A. *Mega Nutrients.* New York, NY: McGraw Hill Books, 1981, 109-110, 150.

LeMarchand, Loic, Jean H. Hankin, Laurence N. Kolonel, and Lynne R. Wilkens. "Vegetable and Fruit Consumption in Relation to Prostate Cancer Risk in Hawaii: A Reevaulation of the Effect of Dietary Beta-Carotene." *American Journal of Epidemiology.* Vol 133, No 3, February 1, 1991, 215-219.

Light, L. "Eat for Health: A Nutrition and Cancer Control Supermarket Intervention." *Public Health Report.* Vol 104, September - October, 1989, 443-450.

Lin, David J. *Free Radicals and Disease Prevention: What You Must Know.* New Canaan, Connecticut: Keats Publishing, Inc., 1993.

Lobstein, D., B.J. Mosbacher, and A.H. Ismail. "Depression as a Powerful Discriminator Between Physically Active and Sedentary Middle Aged Men." *Journal Psychosom Res.* Vol 27, 1983, 69-76.

McGrath, Ellen. *When Feeling Bad Is Good.* New York: Bantam Books, 1992.

Mandino, Og. *The Greatest Miracle in the World.* New York: Bantam Books, 1975.

Mansell, P. and J.P.D. Reckless. "Garlic, Effects on Serum Lipids, Blood Pressure, Coagulation, Platelet Aggregation, and Vasodilation." *British Journal of Medicine.* Vol 303, 1991, 3797.

Mayo Clinic Health Letter. "Fruits and Vegetables: Eat Five Everyday." Vol 10, No 7, July 1992, 1-3.

McMahon, F. G. and Ramon Vargas. "Can Garlic Lower Blood Pressure? A Pilot Study." *Pharmacotherapy.* Vol 13, No 4, 1993, 406-407.

Medical Tribune. "Garlic, Cauliflower, and Soy Sauce Combat Cancer." September 24, 1994, 34.

Menkes, M.S., et al. "Serum Beta Caroene, Vitamins C and E, Selenium, and the Risk of Lung Cancer. New England Journal of Medicine. Vol 315, 1986, 1250-1254.

Mills, P.K., L. Beeson, R.L. Phillips, et al., "Cohort Study of Diet, Lifestyle & Prostate Cancer in Adventist Men." *Cancer* Vol. 64, 1989, 598-604

Mortor, M.Ted *Your Health, Your Choice* Hollywood, FL: Fell Publishers, Inc. 1990

Mowrey, Daniel B. *The Scientific Validation of Herbal Medicine.* New Canaan, Connecticut: Keats Publishing, Inc. 1986.

Murray, Frank, Ed. "Vitamins/Supplements: Garlic, Cancer's Freshest Enemy." *Better Nutrition for Today's Living.* Vol 56, No 8, August 1994, 56-60.

Nagai, K. "Experimental Studies on the Preventive Effect of Garlic Extract Against Infection with Influenza Virus." *Japanese Journal of the Association for Infectious Diseases.* Vol 47, 1973, 111-115.

Napier, Kristine. "Cancer-Fighting Foods: Green Revolution." *Harvard Health Letter.* April 1995, 9-12.

National Adolescent Student Health Survey. American School Health Association, Association for the Advancement of Health Education, Society for Public Health Educators. Oakland, CA: Third Party Publishing Co., 1989.

Neill, Kweethai and Diane D. Allensworth. "A Model to Increase Consumption of Fruit and Vegetables by Implementing the "5-A-Day: Initiative." *Journal of School Health.* Vol 64, No 4, April 1994, 150-155.

New York Times. December 11, 1991, C16.

Bibliography

Page, Lot P. "Epidemiologic Evidence on the Etiology of Human Hypertension and Its Possible Prevention." *American Heart Journal.* Vol 91, 1976, 527-524.

Petkov, V. "Plants and Hypotensive, Antiatheromatous and Coronary Dilating Action." *American Journal of Chinese Medicine.* Vol 7, No 3, 1979, 197-236.

Pharmacotherapy. Vol 13, 1993, 406-407.

Phillips, R.L., F.R. Lemon, W.L. Beeson et al. "Coronary Heart Disease Mortality Among Seventh-Day Adventist with Differing Dietary Habits: A Preliminary Report." *American Journal of Clinical Nutrition.* Vol. 31, 1978, S191

Prabhala, R.H. "Immunomodulation in Humans Caused by Beta-Carotene and Vitamin A." *Nutritional Research.* Vol 10, 1990, 1473-1486.

The Practical Encyclopedia of Natural Healing. Emmaus, PA: Rodale Press, Inc., 1983.

Quillin, Patrick. *Healing Nutrients.* Chicago: Contemporary Books, 1987.

Raloff, J. "A Soy Sauce Surprise." *Science News.* Vol 139, 1991, 357.

Rector-Page, Linda G. *Healthy Healing: An Alternative Healing Reference.* Healthy Healing Publications, 1992.

Robertson, J.M., et al. "A Possible Role for Vitamins C and E in Cataract Prevention." *American Journal of Clinical Nutrition.* Vol 53, 1991, 346S-351S.

Rosenthal, Norman. "Seasonal Affective Disorder." *The Archives of General Psychiatry.* Vol 41, 1984.

Rosenthal, Norman. *Seasons of the Mind.* New York: The Guilford Press, 1989.

Sable-Amplis, R. "Further Studies on the Cholesterol-Lowering Effect of Apples on Humans: Biochemical Mechanisms Involved." *Nutrition Research.* Vol 3, 1983, 325-328.

Sacks, F.M., Bernard Rosner, and Edward H. Kass. "Blood Pressure in Vegetarians." *American Journal of Epidemiology.* Vol 100, 1974. 309-398.

Sacks, F.M., Bernard Rosner, and Edward H. Kass. "Effects of Ingestion of Meat on Plasma Cholesterol of Vegetarians." *Journal of American Medical Association.* Vol 246, 1981, 640-644.

Sainani, G.S., D.B. Desai, and K.N. More. "Onion, Garlic, and Atherosclerosis." *The Lancet.* Sept 11, 1976, 575-576.

Salaman, Maureen and James F. Scheer. *Foods that Heal.* Menlo Park, CA: M.K.S., Inc., 1994.

Sanders, C.L. "Twenty-Nine Ways to Get Your Children to Eat More Vegetables." *Your Life and Health.* August 1982, 18-19.

Schardt, David. "Phytochemicals: Plants Against Cancer." *Nutrition Action Health Letter.* Vol 21, No 3, April 1994, 1, 9.

Seligman, Marty. *Learned Optimism.* New York: Alfred A. Knopf, 1991.

Sharma, V.D., M.S. Sethi, A. Kumar, and J.R. Rarota. "Antibacterial Property of Allium sativum Linn: In Vivo and In Vitro Studies." *Indian Journal of Experimental Biology.* Vol 15, No 6, 1977, 466-468.

Shekelle, R.B. et al. "Dietary Vitamin A and Risk of Cancer in the Western Electric Study." *The Lancet.* Vol. 2, 1981, 1185-1190.

Sherry, Michael M. *Confronting Cancer: How to Care for Today and Tomorrow.* New York: Insight Books, Plenum Press, 1994.

Sriniviesan, M.R., K. Sambaiah, M.N. Satyanarayana, and M.V.L. Rao. "Influence of Red Pepper and Capsaicin on Growth, Blood Constituents, and Nitrogen Levels in Rats." *Nutrition Reports.* Vol 21, No 3, 1980, 455-467.

Stern, G.M. "Vitamin E and Parkinson's Disease." *The Lancet.* Vol 1, 1987, 508.

Stoll, A. and E. Seebeck. "Chemical Investigations of Allicin, the Specific Principle of Garlic." *Advances in Enzymology.* Vol 11, 1951, 377.

Subar, Amy F., Linda C. Harlan, and Margaret E. Mattson. "Food and Nutrient Intake Differences Between Smokers and Non-smokers in the US." *American Journal of Public Health.* Vol 80, No 11, November 1990, 1323-1329.

Surgeon General Report on Health and Nutrition. Washington, D.C.: U.S. Dept. of Health and Human Services, 1988. DHHS (PHS) Publication #88-50210.

Times-Dispatch. Richmond, Virginia. "Cancer Fighter Is Found in Broccoli." March 15, 1992.

Toh, C.C., T.S. Lee, and A.K. Kiang. "The Pharmacological Actions of Capsaicin and Analogues." *British Journal of Pharmacology.* Vol 10, 1955, 175-182.

Bibliography

Trock, Bruce, Elaine Lanze, Peter Greenwald. "Review: Dietary Fiber, Vegetables, and Colon Cancer: Critical Review and Meta-Analyses of the Epidemiologic Evidence." *Journal of the National Cancer Institute.* Vol 82, No 8, April 18, 1990, 650-661.

University of Califorina at Berkeley Wellness Letter: *The Newsletter of Nutrition, Fitness, and Stress Management.* "Wellness Facts." Vol 12, Issue 2, November 1995.

Varma, Shambhu D., "Scientific Basis for Medical Therapy of Cataracts by Antioxidants." *American Journal of Clinical Nutrition.* Vol 23, 1991, 335S-345S.

Verpoorte, R. "Some Phytochemical Aspects of Medicinal Plant Research." *Journal of Ethnopharmacology.* Vol 25, 1989, 43-59.

Walker, W.J. and B.N. Brin. "U.S. Lung Cancer Mortality and Declining Cigarette Tobacco Consumption." *J Clin Epidemiol.* Vol 41, 1988, 179-185.

Weisburger, J.H. "Causes, Relevant Mechanisms, and Prevention of Large Bowel Cancer." *Semin Oncol.* Vol 18, 1991, 216-336.

Werloach, M. *Healing Through Nutrition.* New York, NY: Harper Collins Publishers, 1993

Werloach, M.R., *Nutritional Influences on Illness*, second edition. Tarzana, CA: Third Line Press, 1993

Whitaker, Julian. *Dr. Whitaker's Guide to Natural Healing.* Rocklin, CA: Prima Publishing, 1995.

Whitty, J.P. and L.F. Bjeldanes. "The Effects of Dietary Cabbage on Xenobiotic-Metabolizing Enzymes and the Binding of Aflatoxin B to Hepatic DNA in Rats." *Food Chem. Toxicol.* Vol 25, 1987, 581-587.

Wijesekera, R.O.B. "Is There An Industrial Future for Phytopharmaceutical Drugs? An Outline of UNIDO Programmes in the Sector." *Journal of Ethnopharmacology.* Vol. 32, 1991, 217-224.

Willett, Walter C. "Relation of Meat, Fat and Fiber Intake to the Risk of Colon Cancer in a Prospective Study Among Women." *New England Journal of Medicine.* Vol 323, 1990, 1664-1672.

Yamada, Y. and K. Azuma. "Evaluation of the In Vitro Antifungal Activity of Allicin." *Antimicrobial Agents Chemotherapy.* Vol 11, 1977, 743.

Yen, Peggy K. "An Apple a Day Is Not Enough." *Geriatric Nursing.* November/December 1992, 336, 339.

You, W.C., W.J. Blot, Y.S. Chang, et al. "Allium Vegetables and Reduced Risk of Stomach Cancer. *Journal of the National Cancer Institute.* Vol 81, 1989, 162-164.

Young, Simon. "Folic Acid and Psychopathology." *Progress in Neuropsychopharmacology and Biological Psychiatry.* Vol 13, 1989, 841-863.

Young, Simon. "Some Effects of Dietary Components (Amino Acids, Carbohydrate, Folic Acid) on Brain Serotonin Synthesis, Mood and Behavior." *Canadian Journal of Physiology and Pharmacology.* Vol 69, 1991, 893-903.

Ziegler, R.G., A.F. Subar, N.E. Craft, G. Ursin, B.L. Patterson, and B.I. Graubard. "Does B-Carotene Explain Why Reduced Cancer Risk is Associated with Vegetable and Fruit Intake?" *Cancer Research.* Vol 52, 1992, 2060s-2066s.

INDEX

3-n-butyl 102
acid
  aminio 113, 114, 116
  artichoke 38
  ellagic 37
  fatty 64
  folic 33, 62-63, 72, 113-114
  galacturonic 108
  retinoic 62
  rosemaric 14
ADA (adenosine deminase) 63
adenosine 39, 45, 46
Aeromonas 49
aflatoxin 40
aging 37, 44, 124, 136
aging process 6, 123, 124
agitation 53,116
AIDS 17, 31, 51-52, 124, 128
ajoene 40, 45, 47
alcohol 58, 101, 123, 135
alfalfa 113
allergy(ies) 3, 7, 41
allicin 45, 49, 51, 52, 63
Allium sativum 90
allyl sulfide 47
allyl trisulfide 48
Aloe 140
Aloe vera 140
alpha-oxide 94
alternative medicine 9
Alzheimer's disease 14
American Cancer Society 27
                                   67, 80
American Research Cancer
Institute 47, 48, 57, 58
amino acid 113, 114, 116
Anderson Cancer Center 47
angina 51, 97-98, 126
antiaging 136
antianxiety 116
antibacterial 45, 48

antibiotic 44, 48, 51-52
antiblood 45
anticholesterol 106
anticlotting 45
antidepressant 114
antihypertensive 100, 102
antithrombotic 45
antibacterial 45, 48
antibiotic 44, 48, 51-52
anticarcinogens 47
anticarcinogenic 90
antidepressants 114
antiflatulent 50
antifungal 45, 52-53
antiinsecticidal 18
antimicrobial properties 18, 53
antiparasitic 18
antioxidant 11, 14, 50, 62, 64
                             72, 75, 121-133
antiviral 18
anxiety 53, 112, 113, 116, 120
apples ... 16, 22, 77, 79, 100, 107
apricots 71, 79, 102
arterial damage 108
arteries ... 14, 38, 50, 97, 99, 105
                                   107, 125
arteriosclerosis 19, 29
artery-clogging 50
arthritis 45, 129
  osteo 45
  rhumatoid 124
artichokes 38
  acid 38
asbestos 67
asparagus 63, 113, 131
aspirin 30, 36, 38, 45
asthma 41, 44, 54, 124
asthma attacks 41
asthma bronchitis 41
atherosclerosis 15, 35, 38,
                                   125-126
avocado(s) 63, 102, 107, 131
Bacillus 49
bacteria 36, 37, 48, 122, 128
bacteriotatic 45

bananas 22, 102
beans 50, 84, 85, 106
  dried 79, 92, 120
  garbanzo 63
  kidney............... 63, 105
  lima 63
  pinto 63, 84, 101
  soy 89
beets............... 63, 85, 89
berries........... 13, 37, 63, 131
beta carotene 13, 32, 35, 62,
  70-71, 72, 73, 76, 88, 97, 131, 132
biological response modifier ... 47
biotechnological industry ... 15-16
bladder.................. 57
  infections................ 37
blood ... 14, 17, 29, 39, 71, 85, 89
  92, 95-108, 114, 115, 125, 126, 127
  cells.................... 63
  cholesterol..... 31, 97, 104-105
  clots 14, 29, 39, 45, 98
  pressure 21, 39, 44, 46, 97,
    98, 100, 101, 102, 124, 136
  purifiers................. 39
  sugar............. 28, 33, 41
  supply 126
  tests............. 39, 40, 71
  vessels 8, 125
blood vessels 46, 125
  constriction............ 8, 102
  dialation 46
blueberries 36
boron 36
bowel movements........... 37
brain........ 30, 38, 99, 112, 113
    114, 115, 117, 118, 129, 136
brainpower 36
breast feeding
broccoli 13, 15, 31, 32, 33, 34
    57, 61, 62, 63, 64, 71, 72, 73, 83,
    86, 100, 101, 102, 131
Brussels sprouts ... 31, 61, 64, 83
    86, 100, 102, 131
bronchial asthma 41
bronchitis......... 30, 41, 49, 67

brown rice 85, 113
Brucella 48
butter 29
cabbage ... 14, 31, 33, 34, 57, 64
    71, 78, 83, 85, 86, 131
calcium 34, 63, 98, 100, 101
caloric intake............... 22
calories 16, 24, 81, 111
cancer ... 8, 13, 15, 19, 23, 29, 31
    32, 35, 36, 40, 47, 56-65, 96, 123
        125, 126, 127, 130
  basal cell skin 93
  bladder 57
  breast 28, 32, 47, 57, 60,
            80-86
  cells.................... 61
  cervix................... 57
  colon 17, 33, 37, 38, 48, 57,
            60, 63, 74-79
  diet and cancer 57
  development 61
  endometrium 57, 75
  esophagus............... 57
  liver..................... 40
  lung..... 29, 30, 31, 32, 48, 57,
            66-73, 74, 127
  mouth 57
  ovary.................... 57
  pancreatic 29, 35, 57, 87-94
  prevention....... 58, 60, 61-62
            63, 64
  prostate.......... 32, 38, 87-89
  rate 57
  risk 57
  skin............... 64, 92-94
  squamous 93
  stomach .. 14, 40, 48, 57, 89-91
  uterine.................. 83
Cancer Research Center...... 29
cantaloupe 62, 100, 102
capsaicin 29, 30, 103, 115
carcinogens ... 31, 47, 61, 62, 63,
            64, 68, 73, 76, 90
cardiovascular
  angina attacks 35

Index

disease 95-108
carotenoids 28, 30, 31, 35, 62
carrots 13, 16, 22, 30, 31, 62
    71, 75, 79, 108, 131
cataracts. ... 31, 35, 124, 128-129
cauliflower ... 31, 62, 83, 100, 102
cayenne 29, 103
cells. ... 29, 30, 31, 32, 37, 61, 62
    121-122, 130
cancer. 61, 86, 89
colon 76
healthy 64, 126
malignant. 47-48
membrane 128
nerve 112
T cells 128
tumor 72
unhealthy 126
central nervous system 38, 40
    116, 129
cervical cancer 57
chemopreventive 13, 31, 60
chemotherapeutic 72
chemotherapy 47, 127
chickpeas 63, 113
chlorophyll 32
cholesterol. . 14, 35, 38, 40, 49, 50
    53, 93, 95, 97, 104, 105, 106, 115,
    116, 125
anticholesterol agent. 106
levels. 31, 36, 38, 40, 49, 50
    102, 103, 104, 105, 106, 107
chromate(s) 67
chromium 33
chronic diseases . 6, 7, 14, 15, 123
cigarettes 67
circulation 14
Citrobacter 49
colds 30, 41, 44, 52
collards 63, 86, 101, 113, 131
colon cancer. .. 17, 33, 37, 38, 48,
    57, 60, 63, 74-79
corn. 85, 114, 140
cough 30, 44
medicines 44

whooping 44, 54
coumarins 28, 35
cruciferous vegetables. . 31, 32-34,
    77-78, 83
cynarin 38
disease(s) ... 8, 13, 16, 44, 56, 58
    67, 82, 87, 124, 125, 130
acute 6
Alzheimer's 14
chronic 6, 7, 14, 15, 123
degenerative 32, 127
infectious 4, 14
heart .. 13, 19, 30, 40, 44, 45, 50
    58, 95-108, 125, 126, 130
neurological 130
Parkinson's 124, 129-130
prevention 16, 134
respiratory 49
sickle cell 130
treatment 135
depression 8, 109-120
DHEA 140
diabetes 19, 33, 44
diallyl disulfide 54, 84
diallyl sulfide 47
diarrhea 36, 49
diphenylthiosulfinate 41
diphtheria 44
disease 8, 11, 44, 56, 58, 82
    87, 124, 130
acute 6
chronic 6-7, 14, 15, 123
degenerative 32, 127
developing 67
fighting 16
heart .. 13, 19, 30, 40, 44, 45, 50
    58, 95, 96, 97, 98, 104-108,
    124, 125, 126, 130
infectious 4, 14
prevention 16, 134
respitory 49
treatment 124-125, 135
diverticulitis 124
DNA 29, 63-64
drugs 4, 5, 106, 128

155

The Facts About Phytochemicals

antibiotic 52
illegal 136
miracle 2
over-the-counter 2, 54
perscription 2, 11
pharmaceutical 4
synthetic 11, 13
drowsiness 36, 40
dysentery 44
E. coli 37
ellagic acid 37
emotions 102, 117
endive 113
endorphins 30, 114, 115, 117
energy 44, 110, 123, 135, 140
enzymes 32, 61, 62, 64
  ADA 63
  phase 2 61
  anticancer 32
Escherichia 49
esophageal cancer 57
estrogen . . . 31, 32, 34, 36, 83, 84
exercise . . . 20, 21, 70, 95, 99, 114
  117, 120, 123, 133, 136
expectorant 30
eyes 35, 39, 93, 99, 128
fat . . . 22, 24, 25, 29, 40, 105, 107
  acids 64
  blocker 39
  diet 76, 82, 89
  intake 75, 77, 81-82, 140
  omega-6 93
  low 107
  monosaturated 107
fatigue . . 44, 53, 110, 116, 118, 119
fatty acid 64
fiber 10, 22, 75, 76, 77, 89, 92
  100, 107, 108
figs 63, 101
flatulence 23, 44, 50
flavonoids 35, 64
flaxseed 16
flu 14, 30, 52
folate 62-63, 72
  SEE FOLIC ACID

folic acid 33, 62-63, 72, 113
food 10, 11, 15, 16, 20, 25, 35
  39, 55, 57, 70, 71, 72, 89, 110, 130
  131
  allergies 7
  antioxidants in 131-133
  designer 15-17
  fast 4, 140
  fatty 29
  food guide pyramid 15, 21
  fried 29, 123
  function 16
  gas producing 50
  health 140
  mold 63
  mood 110, 112-116, 118
  nutritious 20, 89, 100-102
  performance 16
  plants 10-11
  preventative 13, 68, 85, 105
  107, 108
  sweet 68
FDA 4
Food Guide Pyramid 15, 21
free radicals 14, 28, 121-133
fried food(s) 29, 123
fruits 11, 14, 15, 18, 19-26, 96
  100, 111, 138
angina preventative 98
blood pressure 99-100, 103
breast cancer preven . . 81, 82, 86
cancer preventative . . . 57, 58, 60
  64, 66-73
cholesterol preventative 105
colon cancer prevent 74-79
depression 112, 115, 117
free radicals 121-133
intake 139-140
phytochemicals 27-42
potassium 102
protstate prevent 87-94
skin cancer prev 87-94
stomach cancer prev 87-94
SAD preventative 120
galacturonic acid 108

Index

garlic ... 16, 39, 41, 43-55, 78, 84
  85, 90, 98, 102, 103, 106, 115, 116
  131
gas 24, 44, 50
gastroenteritis 49
gastrointestinal 48
genetic(s) 130
  coding 32, 62, 125
  messages 63
  mutation 32
  pattern 61
genus Brassica 31
germanium 43
Giardia lamblia 52
Ginkgo biloba 14
glucarate 35, 38
glutathione 35
glutathione-S-transferase 64
gout 36
grapefruit 34-35, 92, 100,
  108, 131
grapes 36-37, 131
green(s) 34, 84
green cabbage 34
green leafy veggies 71, 73, 86
green peas 16, 100, 113
green tea 13
green tea polyphenols 14
guaifensein 30
guava 100
H. pylori bacteria 48
Hafnia 49
Hawthorn berry extract 14
hay fever 30, 41
HCL (hydrochloride) 89
HDL levels 36, 40, 50, 104,
  105, 106
healing 5, 8, 50, 96, 136
  garlic healing properties ... 43-55
  natural 3, 5, 7, 9, 53, 140
  plants 11
health ... 1, 3, 5, 6-7, 9, 12, 13, 15
  19, 20, 21, 22, 24, 26, 55, 61, 63,
  65, 90, 108, 123, 124, 126, 133,
  134-140

benefits ... 3, 14-15, 18, 58, 132
care 1, 2, 5, 7, 9, 13, 51, 59
care costs 2
diet 21, 22, 59
food 116, 118
holistic 7
info 39
insurance 1
magazines 13
mental 110
newsletter 121
problems 130
standards 12
heart .. 8, 14, 35, 79, 95, 126, 136
  American Heart Assn 30, 96
  attack(s) ... 8, 45, 51, 96, 97, 98
    99, 104, 105, 108, 125
  disease 13, 19, 30, 40, 44,
    45, 50, 58, 95, 96, 97, 98-99, 104
    105, 106, 124, 125, 126, 130
  failure 99
  pain 97
  patients 51
  problems 95-108
HIV 17
hookworms 49
hormone(s) .. 8, 31-32, 44, 64, 119
  benign 32
  dependent cancers 83
  destructive 8
  melatonin 119
  parathyroid 101
  production 123
  steriodal 38
  stress 102, 114
hot peppers 29-30
  SEE CAPSAICIN
immune system . 8, 48, 51, 54, 128
  function 8
  response 31, 128
  immunological defense 72
indigestion 44
indole 34, 64, 73, 77, 83
indole-3-carbinol ... 31, 32, 83, 86
infection 8, 37, 44, 48, 49, 123

157

bladder................. 37
ear..................... 54
lung.................... 51
secondary............... 51
urinary tract........... 49
viral................... 128
wound................... 49
infectious diseases...... 4, 14
influenza............... 52
insulin................. 19, 33
synthesis............... 41
interleukin............. 8, 48
intestines.............. 52, 75
parasites............... 52
worms................... 49
irritability............ 53, 113, 116
isothiocyanate.......... 32
SEE PHENETHYL ISOTHIOCYANATE
kale.... 31, 33, 61, 62, 63, 64, 71, 83, 101, 131
kidney.................. 99
kidney beans............ 63, 105
kiwi fruit.............. 100
Klebsiella.............. 49
Kwai.................... 102, 103
L-phenylalanine......... 116
L-tyrosine.............. 116
LDL levels.... 36, 38, 50, 97, 104, 105, 107, 125
lead.................... 17
legumes................. 22, 77, 79, 92, 106
lemons.................. 34-35
lentils................. 113
lettuce................. 16, 22, 71, 131
licorice root........... 16
light box............... 119
lima beans.............. 63
limonoids............... 35
liver................... 28, 50
cancer.............. 40, 48
cells............... 64
function............ 38
stimulation......... 28
lung(s)........ 41, 67, 68, 71, 98
cancer... 29, 30, 31, 32, 48, 57, 66-73, 74, 127
infections.............. 51
tumors.................. 86
lutein.................. 32, 73
lycopene...... 28, 29, 73, 88, 92
SEE TOMATOES
Lycopesicon esculentum...... 28
SEE TOMATOES
macrobiotic diet........ 103, 106
macrophages............. 48
malignant cells......... 47-48
mango(es)............... 35
melanoma................ 40, 93
melatonin............... 119
meningitis.............. 53
menopause...... 36, 80, 81, 105
mental.................. 7-8
alertness............... 36
health professional..... 110, 119
outlook................. 135
stress.................. 102
metabolic balancing..... 111
metabolism....... 15, 31, 47, 83
metastasis.............. 86
methyl allyl trisulfide......... 46
milk............ 34, 46, 48, 101
minerals................ 12
trace................... 33
molecules...... 61, 122, 130-131
moles................... 93
mood(s)......... 7, 30, 53, 110, 112, 113, 115
disorders............... 120
swings.................. 118
mucilage................ 43
muscle(s)....... 46, 95, 123, 136
relaxer............. 39, 46
National Cancer Institute... 14, 16, 17, 23, 40
natural healing.. 3, 5, 7, 9, 53, 140
neurotransmitters....... 112-113
nickle chromates........ 67
nicorette gum........... 69
nitrosamines............ 40
nutriceuticals.......... 16

Index

nutrients........ 19, 68, 111, 112
                            126, 127
nutrition.... 16, 48, 57, 63, 74, 75
                               89, 112
  depletion................. 109
  difficiency 111
  experts................... 19
  nutritional methods.......... 3
  nutritious foods .. 16, 20, 26, 136
  problems 19
  research.................. 15
  school lunches 24
  students, effect on 24
  study 24
  supplements............... 17
  value.................. 12, 20
oat bran 100
okra 62, 63, 101
olive oil............... 89, 107
oltipraz 64
omega-6 fats................ 93
onions... 39-41, 43, 63, 85, 90, 98
  anti-anxiety agent 116
  anti-oxidant............... 98
  cholesterol fighting 106
  Vidalia 90
orange(s) ... 16, 22, 34-35, 63, 71
               72, 73, 92, 100, 131
  juice 17, 68, 101-102
osteoporosis............ 34, 36
ovarian cancer 57
over-the-counter drugs
overweight 99
  men 75
  women 81
oxidative process 123
pancreas.................. 57
  pancreatic cancer.... 29, 35, 57,
                              87-94
  panceatitis 124
papaya.......... 35-36, 88, 108
parasite(s).............. 49, 52
  antiparasitic 18
parathyroid 102
Parkinson's disease........ 124,
                              129-130
parents................... 25
parsley................... 62
passive smoking............ 67
peaches 71
peanuts 85
pears 16, 77, 79
peas 16, 85, 100, 113
pectin........ 35, 38, 78-79, 107
penicillin............... 37, 51
pepper(s) 131
  cayenne 103
  chili............. 114-115, 131
  hot peppers............ 29-30
  red pepper 100
                   SEE CAPSAICIN
peptic ulcers.............. 122
pesticide(s)............ 17, 123
pharmaceutical(s) .. 2, 3, 4, 10, 11
                               12, 41
  companies............. 3, 4-5
  phytopharmaceuticals....... 12
  phase 2 enzymes 61
  phenethyl isothiocyanate...... 32
        SEE ALSO ISOTHIOCYANATE
  phenols................... 34
  polyphenol 14
phytoalexins............... 63
phytochemical(s)... 10, 12, 13-14,
    16, 17, 18, 22, 27-42, 56, 58, 60,
    61, 62, 64, 72, 73, 78, 83, 84, 85,
    88, 90, 102, 103, 106, 107, 115,
                    116, 122, 139
  chemistry.............. 12-13
  components 107
  compounds 11, 13, 29
  study of 14-15, 16
phytoestrogen.............. 84
phytogenic substances 16
pineal gland 119
pinworms 49
pipe (smoking)
plaque 14, 97, 105, 125, 126
platelets 45, 98
pneumonia 44, 49

159

The Facts About Phytochemicals

pollution 67, 123
polyps 33, 63, 76-77
potassium 101-102
potato 62, 113
prednisone 41
premature aging...... SEE AGING
prescription drugs 2, 11
prevention 1-9, 18, 120, 127
130, 136
blood clotting 98
cancer 29, 31, 35, 56-65, 68
72, 73, 75, 77, 80-86
cataracts................ 128
depression 114
disease.............. 16, 125
prostaglandin(s) 54
A1...................... 39
E 39
prostate cancer 32, 38, 87-89
protease inhibitors........... 92
Proteus................... 49
Providencia................ 49
prunes 79, 102
quercetin 36, 40, 41, 47, 116
Questran.................. 14
radish(es) 61
raisins................... 102
raspberries 36
red grapes .... SEE GRAPES
remedies 5, 7, 9, 11, 74
respiratory problems 44, 49
retinoic acid 62
rheumatoid arthritis 124
ringworms................. 49
rosemarinic acid 14
roundworms 49
S-allyl cysteine 84
salads............. 20, 22, 105
salicylates................. 38
Salmonella 49
salt.............. 24, 100-101
seafood............... 89, 103
Seasonal Affective Disorder (SAD)
.... 109-120
secondary infections 51

sedative 40, 116
selenium 44, 85, 131, 132
self-care 134
self-help 111
self-medication 118
senility 124
serotonin
sickle cell disease... SEE DISEASE
sinusitis................ 30, 49
skin
abscesses 48
cancer 40, 64, 71, 92-94
rashes 44
smoking........... 67-71, 123
passive.................. 67
sodium.............. 100-101
soybeans 89
spinach.......... 62-63, 71, 73,
102, 114, 131
spirit..................... 8
spirituality 7, 95, 136, 138
Spirulina 14
split peas............ SEE PEAS
squamous cell cancer 93
Staphylococcus............. 48
steroidal horrmones 38
stomach
cancer 14, 40, 48, 57, 89-91
lining 29-30, 54
ulcer.................... 33
stomach lining
strawberries........ 36, 100, 108
Strepacoccus 48
stress........ 8-9, 102, 113, 114,
120, 135
hormone(s) 102, 114
stroke(s) 19, 31, 45, 97, 99
100, 101, 124
sulforaphane............... 32
sulfur 28
sunburn 93
sweet potato(es) 131
synovial sac 129
T-cells................... 128
T-helper cell 31

160

Index

T-lymphocytes............. 48
tamoxifen................. 83
tangerines................ 35
tap water................ 117
tapeworms................. 49
terpenes.................. 35
throat.................... 48
thromboxane............... 45
tomato(es).. 22, 27, 28-29, 30, 72, 85, 88, 92, 100, 102, 131
tooth decay............. 17, 37
trace mineral............. 33
tuberculosis.......... 44, 51, 54
turnip(s).......... 31, 34, 83, 86
  greens............ 62-63, 101
typhoid fever............. 49
typhus................. 44, 54
ulcers................. 14, 54
  stomach................ 33
  peptic................ 122
ultraviolet
  lighting........... 123, 128
  rays................... 93
uranium................... 67
urinary tract
  infection.............. 49
USDA..................... 14
uterine cancer............ 83
vaginal yeast infection........ 52
vegetable(s)
  cruciferous 31, 32-34, 77-78, 83
  oil.................... 98
vegetarian(s).............. 70
  and heart disease......... 96
Vibrio................... 49
Vidalia onion............. 90
vinyl chloride............ 67
viral infection.......... 128
virus
  influenza............... 52
vitamin(s) 12, 13, 60
vitamin A................ 14
vitamin C...... 35, 68-69, 82, 94, 97, 100, 108, 115, 131, 132

vitamin D................ 89
vitamin E 94, 97, 98, 108, 131, 132
volatile oil............... 43
walnuts
water.............. 52, 75, 85
  tap................... 117
watermelon........... 92, 131
wheat
  bran.................. 100
  bran fiber.............. 76
  bran flakes............. 75
  whole wheat......... 85, 113
whooping cough........ 44, 54
World Cancer Research Fund.. 57
worms.................... 49
yeast infection............ 52

161

APPENDIX A

WHERE TO GET THE PHYTOCHEMICAL PRODUCTS SIMILAR TO THOSE MENTIONED IN THE RESEARCH IN THIS BOOK:

I. MANNATECH INCORPORATED
    2010 North Highway 360
    Grand Prairie, TX 75050
    (214) 641-8829 • (800) 267-2722
    Fax (214) 641-8776 * Fax for Orders (800) 267-2722

A. Phyt-Aloe™ is a capsule filled with flash-dried fruits and vegetables (broccoli, Brussels sprouts, caggabe, carrots, cauliflower, garlic, kale, onions, papaya, pineapple, tomatoes, turnips) and a patented Aloe vera extract (Manapol®).

B. Phyto-Bears™ are a "new generation of Gummi Bears." These delightful bears contain the same ingredients as Phyto-Aloe™, but are in delicious Gummi Bear form and flavor. An excellent way to make sure your children get those fruits and vegetables they need!

II. NEW LIFE NUTRICEUTICALS
    P. O. Box 996
    Boca Raton, FL 33429
    (407) 391-6844

All inquiries and orders for:
**DESIGNING YOUR LIFE WITH DESIGNER FOODS:
THE FACTS ABOUT PHYTOCHEMICALS, or**

**THE MIRACLE IN ALOE VERA:
THE FACTS ABOUT POLYMANNANS, or**

**BOUNTIFUL HEALTH, BOUNDLESS ENERGY,
BRILLIANT YOUTH: THE FACTS ABOUT DHEA**

Should be addressed to:
CHARIS PUBLISHING COMPANY
P. O. BOX 740607 • DALLAS, TX 75374
(214) 342-1137 • FAX (214) 343-9058

SINGLE BOOK PRICE ....$12.95 EACH
TWO TO 20 COPIES ....9.95 EACH
OVER 20 COPIES. .... 8.95 EACH
100 + COPIES. ....7.95 EACH

PLEASE SEND _____ COPIES @ $ _____ $ _____

TEXAS RESIDENTS ADD 8.25% TAX $ _____

SHIPPING AND HANDLING (SEE BELOW) $ _____

    1 Book — $2.25
    2-20 Books — $1 per book
    Over 20 Books — 70¢ per book

TOTAL AMOUNT ENCLOSED $ _____

SHIPPING INFORMATION:
NAME _____

ADDRESS _____

CITY, STATE, ZIP _____

HOME PHONE _____

WORK PHONE _____